PRAISE FOR A BOOK OF PROVOCATIONS

"Matt Fletcher has created a visual tour de force with *A Book of Provocations*. As an English teacher myself, this resource is brimming with potential, full of images and questions that are sure to stir the curiosity in any classroom."

TREVOR MACKENZIE. AUTHOR OF *DIVE INTO INQUIRY* AND THE *INQUIRY MINDSET SERIES.*

PRAISE FOR A BOOK OF PROVOCATIONS

"Becoming fluent in the language of curiosity means playing with questions, exploring the variance in tone and arrangement of words, observing the variety of ways we can explore a single concept through multiple vantage points, and noticing the impact this 'new dialect' has on the community of learners. *A Book of Provocations* gives its readers scaffolded support in building this language, and Matt models possible frameworks of thinking as we design towards cultures of curiosity in our schools and classrooms. Whether you are new to a practice of inquiry, needing a bit of inspiration, or looking for a stretch in your practice as you approach provocation throughout the cycle of inquiry, be sure you have *A Book of Provocations* on your shelf, ready to grab when the need arises!"

JESSICA VANCE. *EDUCATIONAL CONSULTANT AND AUTHOR OF LEADING WITH A LENS OF INQUIRY: CULTIVATING CONDITIONS FOR ADVANCING CURIOSITY AND EMPOWERING AGENCY*

EDUCATOR'S INSIGHTS

The impact of "A Book of Provocations" has reached far and wide, with its use spreading to classrooms throughout the globe. Teachers from various disciplines and educational settings have embraced the book, utilizing its content to enhance their instructional strategies. The trials and tests conducted by these educators have revealed significant benefits, including heightened student engagement, improved critical thinking skills, and a more vibrant learning atmosphere. The experiences and reflections shared by these teachers underscore the book's ability to inspire innovative teaching practices and enrich the overall educational experience. I am excited to present their stories and insights, illustrating the global influence and transformative power of "A Book of Provocations.

EDUCATOR'S INSIGHTS

"My students described it as 'cool' and 'inspirational'. Matt Fletcher has compiled a first-class resource bank of thought-provoking questions paired with captivating images. With tips on how to motivate the class across all disciplines, it's a must-have for teachers everywhere. We're already excited for volume 2."

OSCAR NOWAK. SECONDARY ENGLISH TEACHER IN CHINA

"I really appreciate how the structured approach of using visual provocations and guiding questions enhanced engagement and learning. It encouraged detailed observation and the use of descriptive language, which led to richer class discussions. The connected role play showed empathy, strong communication skills, and understanding of diverse perspectives. Overall, the activities promoted active learning and collaboration, making complex concepts accessible and engaging for young students."

KARIN ALBERS. PYP COORDINATOR IN THE NETHERLANDS

"The ideas and images in this book are easily adaptable for our MYP language and literature students. Whether an English teacher seeks a step-by-step guide for image analysis or innovative ideas to enhance teaching moments, A Book of Provocations serves as a valuable resource for supporting students in literature or English classes."

MATTHEW KLOOSTERMAN. SECONDARY ENGLISH TEACHER IN CHINA.

"As the aim of a provocation is to build students' curiosity and intellectual interest in a certain topic or concept, creating engaging and meaningful provocations can be demanding for teachers. This book can alleviate some of that burden by offering numerous examples of visual provocations, along with relevant questions, spanning various units of inquiry themes. It is a valuable tool for planning provocations, effectively directing students' interest, and gathering data on their initial conceptions. Moreover, the plans are easy to follow and adaptable to a class's culture, making this resource particularly reliable for teachers looking to develop a repertoire of provocative inquiry tools."

MOHAMMAD HAMMOUR. HOMEROOM TEACHER (SCIENCE, MATH, LANGUAGE ARTS AND SOCIAL STUDIES) IN QATAR.

"As a primary teacher, capturing young students' imaginations is key. *A Book of Provocations* offers wonderfully creative and age-appropriate visual prompts. I used a provocation about different cultural celebrations, and the children were enthralled. They shared their own experiences and asked many questions, which led to a deeper understanding of cultural diversity. This book has been a great help in making learning interactive and engaging, and it's so easy to use and adapt for different themes."

SHALINA PATEL. YEAR 4 PRIMARY SCHOOL TEACHER IN THE U.K.

"I teach IB Language and Literature, and *A Book of Provocations* has been a fantastic addition to my toolkit. The variety of visual provocations and accompanying questions have helped my students develop critical thinking and analytical skills. For instance, the provocation involving dystopian imagery led to an insightful discussion on societal structures and individual freedom, perfectly aligning with our study of dystopian literature. The adaptability of the provocations to suit different classroom cultures makes this book a reliable and versatile resource."

EDUCATOR'S INSIGHTS

STEVEN CARTER. IB LANGUAGE AND LITERATURE TEACHER IN JAPAN.

"A Book of Provocations has been instrumental in enriching my science lessons. The visual provocations were easily relatable to environmental science and were extremely impactful. I really enjoyed the five main themes covered in the book and found that the images were supportive in connecting real-world content to what we study in class. The students were immediately engaged and motivated to learn more about how they can help protect the environment. The book's well-organized and adaptable plans have made lesson planning much more efficient and effective."

GEMMA HARTLEY. GRADE 5 PRIMARY SCHOOL TEACHER IN SPAIN

"A Book of Provocations has been a game-changer in my history classes. The visual prompts and questions are perfect for sparking critical thinking and in-depth discussions. My students used the images to make connections to historical events and explore various cultural contexts, enriching their understanding of the past. This book is an essential tool for any history teacher aiming to inspire curiosity and analytical skills in their students."

JOANNA FISHER. HIGH SCHOOL HISTORY TEACHER IN SINGAPORE

A BOOK OF PROVOCATIONS
VOLUME 1

MATT FLETCHER

LORTHEW
— PRESS —

CONTENTS

Introduction   15

PART ONE
HUMAN INGENUITY
Futuristic Operation   23
Nighttime Symphony   27
Harmony of Innovation   31
Tidal Force   35
Dawn of Illumination   39
Solitary Human   43
Generations Connected   47
Echoes of the Past   51
Waters of Wellness   55
The Future of Fitness   59

PART TWO
SOCIAL ORGANISATION
Unity in Growth   65
Harmony in Care   69
Blueprint for Change   73
Festival Foundations   77
Urban Tranquility   81
Rural Reach   85
Empowering Communities   89
Prepared Together   93
Voices for Change   97
Urban Oasis   101

PART THREE
EXPERIENCES
Journey of Discovery   107
New Horizons   111
The Final Stretch   115
Realm of Silence   119
Tomorrow's Classroom   123

Crossing Cultures	127
City Serenades	131
Canvas of Light	135
Forest Serenity	139
Time to Relax	143

PART FOUR
SHARING THE PLANET

Flow of the Future	149
Seeds of Renewal	153
Tides of Change	157
Guardians of Green	161
Voices of Silence	165
Green in the City	169
Horizons of Hope	173
Desert Innovation	177
Plastic Shells	181
Reversed Realities	185

PART FIVE
IDENTITIES

Before the Chords	191
Symphony of Cultures	195
Extreme Experiences	199
Screens of Self	203
Canvas of Community	207
Silent Greetings	211
Worlds of Work	215
Colors of Health	219
Reflecting	223
Echoes of Time	227

LESSON IDEAS

Predict the Image	233
Observing and Describing Images	237
Creative Writing: Write the Caption	241
Deeper Understanding	245
Questions, Questions, Questions	247
Role-Playing & Debates	251
Cultural & Social Analysis	255

Vocabulary Building	259
Creating AI Images	263
Collaborative Stories	267
Conclusion	271
Also by Matt Fletcher	273
About the Author	275

A Book of Provocations

Copyright © 2024 Matt Fletcher All rights reserved

No part of this publication may be produced in any form or by any electronic or mechanical means, including information storage and retrieval systems without permission.

For information regarding permission, contact the author at www.matttfletcher.com

For inquiries and details, contact the publisher:

www.lorthewpress.co.uk

Published by Lorthew Press

Paperback ISBN:978-1-0686692-4-8

Paperback (BW Edition) ISBN:978-1-0686692-3-1

eBook ISBN: 978-1-0686692-2-4

LORTHEW
— PRESS —

Dedication

To my beautiful wife and daughter, who are my constant support and greatest encouragement. Thank you for being my inspiration every single day.

INTRODUCTION

Welcome to Volume 1 of "A Book of Provocations" — your indispensable resource for cultivating an environment of curiosity, wonder, and enriched conversation in the classroom. With over a decade of experience teaching English, I have consistently observed that the most profound learning occurs when students are engaged by compelling questions and visual stimuli. This insight sparked the creation of this book, designed to ignite minds and inspire dialogue across diverse subjects. Whether exploring new languages or deepening understanding in familiar ones, the use of provocations as a teaching tool has proven invaluable. This approach not only facilitates a deeper engagement with content but also enhances the educational journey by encouraging students to explore, question, and connect more deeply with the material. By integrating my passion for teaching with my commitment to fostering an explorative learning atmosphere, this book aims to transform traditional classroom dynamics and encourage a vibrant exchange of ideas.

INTRODUCTION

Crafting a Dynamic Learning Tool

This book is designed to enrich any educational environment, offering a series of visual provocations that bolster questioning, thinking, and presenting skills. Each provocation starts with an engaging title and three curiosity-provoking questions designed to stimulate students' predictions about the image before they see it. This is followed by a high-quality image with a detailed caption, there is also a QR code for each image on each page allowing you to share, project and download the image. Each image is then accompanied by ten thought-provoking exploratory questions, fostering dynamic dialogue among students and encouraging deeper learning. All images are available as high-quality prints and PDFs on my website. Visit www.matttfletcher.com for more resources.

Navigating a Visual World

In our visual-centric society, the ability to analyze images, discuss their broader implications, and draw connections to overarching themes is invaluable. This book leverages the power of visual media to stimulate curiosity, facilitate debate, and foster deep discussions among students of all ages. It is organized around five key themes —Human Ingenuity, Experiences, Social Organization, Identities, and Sharing the Planet. These themes offer a global perspective and everyday relevance, making them ideal for engaging students in meaningful discourse across numerous subjects.

This book is designed to be flexible and can be adapted to a variety of teaching styles and classroom situations. While it offers a broad spectrum of uses, I have personally found great success in applying the images and content in several impactful ways. The methods listed below are tried and tested, each fostering unique skills and insights among students. Whether you're looking to enhance vocabulary, stimulate critical thinking, or encourage cultural empathy, these approaches can be tailored to fit your specific educational needs and objectives.

Initial Description:

- Present a detailed image to the students. Ask them to list approximately ten observations about the image within 3-5 minutes, enhancing vocabulary and communication skills.

Deeper Understanding:

- Use the provided questions to guide an in-depth exploration of the image's subjects.
- Foster discussions to improve speaking and listening competencies, with students working collaboratively to expand upon each other's ideas.

Question Formulation:

- Encourage students to formulate their own questions or use the image as a springboard for inquiry-based projects.

Role-Playing and Debates:

- Assign roles related to the image's characters or elements.
- Organize role-playing or debates to defend various perspectives, fostering critical thinking and empathy.

Cultural and Social Analysis:

- Select images depicting diverse cultural or social contexts.
- Discuss these settings, prompting students to draw comparisons with their own experiences, thereby promoting global awareness and intercultural understanding.

INTRODUCTION

Vocabulary Building:

- Develop vocabulary lists from the discussions.
- Integrate exercises like matching words to definitions, using new words in sentences, or creating word maps.
- Reinforce vocabulary through its application in various speaking and writing activities.
- Conduct writing races whereby students write down as many words that they know within the picture.

By implementing these strategies, you can utilize *A Book of Provocations* to its fullest potential, creating a dynamic and engaging learning environment for your students. This book offers incredible flexibility, making it a valuable resource in multiple ways.

As you move through the book, you will notice blank white spaces provided for you to take notes, record your thoughts, and list any wonderings that occur. These spaces are designed to encourage reflection and personalization, making the book a practical tool for both teachers and students.

At the back of the book, you will find 10 lesson plan templates to help you deliver some of these ideas mentioned above in your classroom. These templates are crafted to streamline your planning process, allowing you to focus more on engaging with your students and less on preparation.

A Book of Provocations can be used in various ways:

• **As a student self-study book:** Providing students with thought-provoking prompts to explore independently.

• **As a teacher's workbook:** Assisting in planning and organizing engaging activities.

• **As a shared class text:** Fostering collaborative learning and discussion.

The way you use it is really up to you. The book's adaptability ensures that it can meet the diverse needs of any classroom, making it an essential tool for fostering curiosity, critical thinking, and a deeper understanding of various subjects.

The visuals and accompanying questions in this book are tools to challenge perceptions, explore diverse viewpoints, and articulate thoughts clearly and persuasively. Teachers will find this book a valuable resource to inspire students, while students will discover new pathways to learning and personal growth.

As you flip through these pages, allow the images to speak to you and your students. Let them challenge you, change you, and above all, inspire you to ask more, know more, and share more. This book is your canvas for creativity and your stage for expression. Embrace the questions they raise and the discussions they spark. Enjoy the exploration and may your journey through these pages lead to many insightful and inspiring discoveries for you and your students.

PART ONE
HUMAN INGENUITY

The ability of humans to innovate, solve problems, and create solutions across various fields, shaping cultures and advancing societies.

FUTURISTIC OPERATION

What kind of advanced technologies do you envision in a "futuristic operation"?

How do you think a futuristic operation will be different from today?

What potential challenges or breakthroughs do you think are involved in such an operation?

FUTURISTIC OPERATION

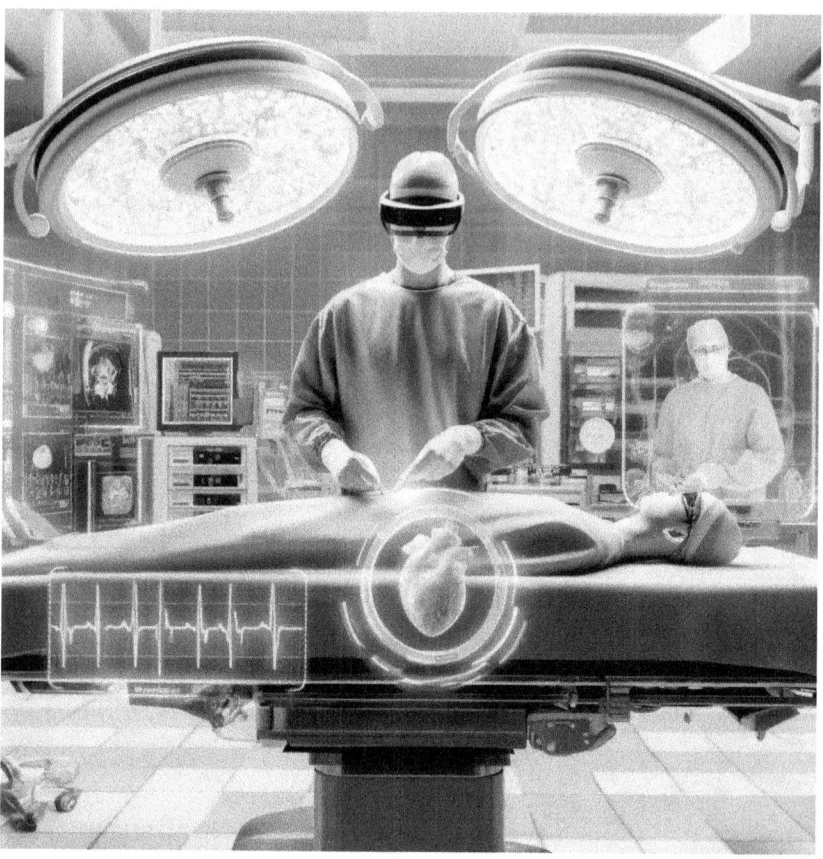

This image showcases a state-of-the-art operating room where a surgeon, using augmented reality glasses, conducts a delicate surgery. The room is equipped with advanced technology, displaying vital signs and medical imaging holographically around the patient.

QUESTIONS FOR EXPLORATION

1. **Enhancing Surgical Precision:** How can augmented reality improve precision in surgical procedures compared to traditional methods?
2. **Impact on Surgeon Training:** What impact does the use of augmented reality have on the training and preparation of surgeons?
3. **Improving Patient Outcomes:** How might real-time access to holographic data during surgery affect patient outcomes?
4. **Cost vs. Benefit:** Considering the high cost of AR technology, how might the investment be justified
5. **Technology Dependence:** Could reliance on augmented reality and other high-tech tools lead to a skills gap in surgeons who may rely too heavily on technology?
6. **Ethical Implications:** What ethical concerns arise from the use of augmented reality in medical settings, particularly regarding patient consent and data security?
7. **Cross-Disciplinary Benefits:** How might developments in AR technology in surgery benefit other fields of medicine?
8. **Technological Failures:** What contingency plans are necessary in surgeries utilizing AR in the event of technological failures?
9. **Global Accessibility:** How can such advanced surgical technologies be made accessible in less developed areas?
10. **Future Innovations:** What future innovations in augmented reality could further transform surgical practices?

FUTURISTIC OPERATION

Notes & Reflections

NIGHTTIME SYMPHONY

What sounds do you associate with a nighttime symphony?

What items of technology might you see in the image?

What emotions or experiences do you connect with the night?

NIGHTTIME SYMPHONY

The scene shows a bustling cityscape at night with drones orchestrating a spectacular light display above. The intricate patterns and designs formed by the drones add a layer of excitement to the city's atmosphere.

QUESTIONS FOR EXPLORATION

1. **Technology and Aesthetics:** How does the use of drone technology in urban landscapes improve or harm the city's aesthetic appeal?
2. **Future Cities:** What are the potential benefits and challenges of incorporating such advanced technology in everyday life?
3. **Privacy and Security:** Could there be privacy or security concerns with the widespread use of drones in populated areas? How might these be addressed?
4. **Environmental Impact:** What environmental impacts might result from the extensive use of light displays and drones in urban areas?
5. **Aerial Photography:** How does the use of drones for aerial photography impact the documentation and preservation of urban landscapes?
6. **Economic Effects:** What economic opportunities could arise from drone light shows and similar technologies? Are there any potential negative economic impacts?
7. **Regulation and Governance:** What kinds of regulations might be necessary to manage the use of drones for entertainment purposes in urban areas?
8. **Public Perception:** How might public perceptions of drones change as their applications in entertainment and other sectors grow?
9. **Technological Accessibility:** How accessible is drone technology for cities around the world? What factors determine its adoption?
10. **Innovation and Creativity:** In what ways could drone technology further evolve to enhance urban entertainment experiences?

NIGHTTIME SYMPHONY

Notes & Reflections

HARMONY OF INNOVATION

How do you imagine different innovations coming together harmoniously?

What kinds of environments or settings do you associate with this title?

What impact do you think such a harmonious blend of innovations could have on society or the world?

HARMONY OF INNOVATION

This landscape image captures a vibrant smart factory floor where collaborative robots (cobots) and human workers of diverse backgrounds seamlessly work together. The scene illustrates the cutting-edge integration of human ingenuity and robotic efficiency in assembling complex machinery.

QUESTIONS FOR EXPLORATION

1. **Workforce Dynamics:** How does the integration of cobots on the factory floor alter workforce dynamics and job roles?
2. **Safety Enhancements:** In what ways could cobots improve safety in manufacturing environments?
3. **Productivity Metrics:** How has the introduction of robots affected the productivity and efficiency of manufacturing processes?
4. **Skills Evolution:** What new skills are required for human workers collaborating with robots, and how can they be developed?
5. **Economic Impact:** What are the economic benefits and challenges of integrating cobots into traditional manufacturing settings?
6. **Ethical Considerations:** Are there ethical concerns regarding the replacement of human jobs with robots, even if partially?
7. **Technological Reliability:** How do manufacturers ensure the reliability and maintenance of cobots in a factory setting?
8. **Global Competition:** How does the adoption of cobot technology affect a country's competitive edge in the global market?
9. **Cultural Adaptation:** How do cultural perceptions of automation and robotics influence the adoption of such technologies in manufacturing?
10. **Future Innovations:** What future advancements in cobot technology could further transform manufacturing industries?

Notes & Reflections

TIDAL FORCE

What natural phenomena do you think might be depicted in an image with this title?

How do you think the concept of a "tidal force" could be represented visually?

What emotions or ideas do you associate with the power and movement of tides?

TIDAL FORCE

This image captures a coastal city's innovative approach to renewable energy through the implementation of giant tidal energy turbines. Engineers of diverse backgrounds are seen on floating platforms, monitoring and managing the energy production.

QUESTIONS FOR EXPLORATION

1. **Efficiency and Output:** How efficient are tidal energy turbines compared to other forms of renewable energy, and what is their energy output potential?
2. **Environmental Impact:** What are the environmental impacts of installing tidal turbines near coastal areas, and how can they be mitigated?
3. **Economic Viability:** Considering the initial investment and maintenance costs, how economically viable is tidal energy for coastal cities?
4. **Technological Challenges:** What are the major technological challenges faced in the implementation and operation of tidal energy turbines?
5. **Community Engagement:** How can local communities be engaged in the planning and benefits of tidal energy projects?
6. **Impact on Marine Life:** What effects do tidal turbines have on marine ecosystems, and how can these effects be minimized?
7. **Policy and Regulation:** What policies and regulations are necessary to support the development and integration of tidal energy solutions?
8. **Global Adoption:** Which other countries are leading in tidal energy, and what can be learned from their experiences?
9. **Future Innovations:** What future innovations in tidal energy technology could increase their adoption and efficiency?
10. **Urban Planning:** How can tidal energy be integrated into urban planning and development strategies to maximize its benefits?

TIDAL FORCE

Notes & Reflections

DAWN OF ILLUMINATION

What images or scenes come to mind when you think of the beginning of illumination?

How might the concept of "illumination" be symbolized in the image?

What changes or transformations do you associate with the dawn of a new era?

DAWN OF ILLUMINATION

This image portrays the momentous occasion in the 18th century when electricity was first demonstrated to a public audience. Set in a grand hall, the scene is bathed in muted tones of black, blue, and grey, highlighting the dramatic effect of glowing light bulbs.

QUESTIONS FOR EXPLORATION

1. **Technological Breakthroughs:** How did the introduction of electricity transform everyday life in the 18th century?
2. **Public Perception:** What were some common misconceptions or fears about electricity when it was first introduced?
3. **Social Impact:** How did electricity influence social structures and daily routines in its early days?
4. **Economic Implications:** What economic changes were prompted by the widespread adoption of electricity?
5. **Cultural Shifts:** How did artists and writers of the time respond to the advent of electricity?
6. **Environmental Considerations:** What were the environmental impacts of early electrical technology?
7. **Political Influence:** How did the introduction of electricity affect political power and the distribution of resources?
8. **Global Spread:** How did the adoption of electricity differ across various countries?
9. **Technological Safety:** What safety concerns were associated with early electrical experiments, and how were they addressed?
10. **Legacy and Evolution:** How have perceptions and uses of electricity evolved from the 18th century to today?

DAWN OF ILLUMINATION

Notes & Reflections

SOLITARY HUMAN

What feelings or thoughts does the idea of being solitary evoke for you?

How do you think the concept of solitude will be visually represented in the image?

What do you imagine about the life or story of a solitary human?

SOLITARY HUMAN

This image captures a lone figure in a space suit standing amidst the ruins of a deserted city. The cityscape, crumbled and overgrown, creates a stark contrast with the modernity of the space suit. This man, holding a simple stick, appears as a symbol of human resilience and adaptability in a post-apocalyptic world where nature reclaims the remnants of civilization.

QUESTIONS FOR EXPLORATION

1. **Symbolism of the Space Suit:** What does the space suit symbolize in this post-apocalyptic scenario?
2. **Role of Nature:** How does the image depict nature's role in reclaiming human-made environments?
3. **Survival Strategies:** What survival strategies might be necessary in such a desolate environment?
4. **Psychological Impact:** What are the psychological impacts of isolation in such a setting?
5. **Technology's Role:** How can technology aid or hinder survival in post-apocalyptic worlds?
6. **Human Resilience:** What does this image suggest about human resilience in the face of environmental collapse?
7. **Ethics of Survival:** What ethical dilemmas might arise when surviving in such conditions?
8. **Historical Lessons:** What historical events or eras could this image be drawing parallels with?
9. **Artistic Expression:** How do the visual elements (lighting, composition) enhance the theme of solitude and decay?
10. **Future Societies:** What might a future society learn from the remnants of this once-thriving city?

Notes & Reflections

GENERATIONS CONNECTED

How do you envision different generations being connected?

What kinds of relationships or interactions do you think might be depicted in the image?

What impact do you think the connections between generations have on society?

GENERATIONS CONNECTED

This image portrays a serene evening in a family's living room where three generations are engaging with modern digital technology. A child, immersed in a virtual reality experience, contrasts with a young adult casually browsing on a tablet and an elderly person enjoying content on a smart TV.

QUESTIONS FOR EXPLORATION

1. **Generational Engagement:** How does each generation's approach to technology differ in this image?
2. **Impact on Communication:** What impact might these technologies have on communication within the family?
3. **Learning Opportunities:** How can different generations learn from each other's tech usage?
4. **Privacy Concerns:** What are the privacy implications of using such diverse technologies within one household?
5. **Social Interaction:** Does technology enhance or hinder social interaction among family members?
6. **Screen Time:** What are the benefits and drawbacks of the varied screen times observed across the generations?
7. **Educational Value:** How can the technologies depicted be used to enhance educational experiences for the child?
8. **Technology Dependency:** What does the image suggest about potential dependencies or addictions to technology?
9. **Cultural Differences:** How might cultural attitudes towards technology influence a family's dynamics as seen in this image?
10. **Future Trends:** What future technological developments could further change how families interact with technology?

GENERATIONS CONNECTED

Notes & Reflections

ECHOES OF THE PAST

What memories or historical events come to mind when you think of "echoes of the past"?

How might the image portray the lingering effects of the past?

What emotions or reflections do you associate with hearing stories from history?

This image presents a virtual reality classroom where students of various backgrounds, equipped with VR headsets, are guided by an AI tutor resembling a real person. They explore a realistically rendered ancient Egyptian tomb, complete with detailed hieroglyphics and artifacts. This setting blends historical exploration with advanced educational technology, offering a unique learning experience.

QUESTIONS FOR EXPLORATION

1. **Educational Impact:** How does virtual reality transform traditional learning environments, especially for historical subjects?
2. **AI as Tutors:** What are the benefits and drawbacks of using AI as tutors in educational settings?
3. **Engagement Levels:** How might VR increase student engagement compared to conventional teaching methods?
4. **Cultural Representation:** How important is accuracy in the cultural representation within VR experiences?
5. **Technology Accessibility:** What steps can be taken to make advanced educational technologies like VR more accessible to underprivileged schools?
6. **Learning Retention:** Does learning through VR improve retention and understanding of complex subjects like history?
7. **Safety and Ethics:** What are the safety and ethical considerations educators should consider when implementing VR in classrooms?
8. **Future of Education:** How could VR change the future landscape of education across different disciplines?
9. **Digital Literacy:** How does using VR in education contribute to students' digital literacy skills?
10. **Parental and Community Reaction:** How might parents and the broader community react to the use of immersive tech like VR for educational purposes?

ECHOES OF THE PAST

Notes & Reflections

WATERS OF WELLNESS

What do you imagine when you think of water as a source of wellness?

How might the image capture the healing or rejuvenating properties of water?

What personal or cultural connections do you have with the idea of wellness through water?

The image depicts a rural scene, where a portable, solar-powered water purification device plays a central role. With only a couple of villagers interacting with the device by the riverbank, the setting is enhanced by traditional village houses in the background. This scene illustrates the critical impact of accessible and sustainable technology on the health and well-being of rural communities.

QUESTIONS FOR EXPLORATION

1. **Technological Impact:** How can solar-powered water purification devices impact the health outcomes of rural communities?
2. **Sustainability:** What are the environmental benefits of using solar-powered technology for communities?
3. **Economic Advantages:** How might such technology affect the economic conditions of a rural community?
4. **Adoption Challenges:** What challenges might communities face when adopting such new technologies?
5. **Technological Adoption:** How do economic factors influence the adoption of solar-powered technologies in rural communities?
6. **Water Quality:** What improvements in water quality can be typically observed with such purification systems?
7. **Maintenance and Training:** What is required to maintain these systems, and how are locals trained to use them?
8. **Long-Term Viability:** How sustainable are solar-powered water purification systems in the long term for rural communities?
9. **Governmental Support:** What role can local or national governments play in facilitating the adoption of these technologies?
10. **Community Engagement:** How important is community engagement in the successful integration of these systems into daily life?

Notes & Reflections

THE FUTURE OF FITNESS

What advancements or innovations do you think will shape the future of fitness?

How might technology be integrated into the fitness routines depicted in the image?

What changes in fitness culture or practices do you envision for the future?

THE FUTURE OF FITNESS

This image showcases an athlete running through a high-tech park, outfitted with advanced wearable devices that monitor real-time health stats. The scene emphasizes the seamless integration of technology and physical activity, as the athlete's biometric sensors display vital data like heart rate, calories burned, and distance traveled. The modern park setting underscores a future where technology enhances every aspect of personal fitness and health.

QUESTIONS FOR EXPLORATION

1. **Technological Integration:** How do wearable devices transform traditional training methods for athletes?
2. **Data Privacy:** What are the implications of real-time data tracking on an individual's privacy?
3. **Performance Enhancement:** How can real-time data provided by wearables directly enhance athletic performance?
4. **Health Monitoring:** In what ways can continuous health monitoring change everyday health management for the average person?
5. **Tech Dependency:** Could there be a downside to becoming overly dependent on technology for fitness and health monitoring?
6. **Accuracy and Reliability:** How accurate and reliable are the health metrics provided by wearable devices, and what improvements are needed?
7. **Accessibility:** How can technology like this be made more accessible to people in different socio-economic groups?
8. **Future Developments:** What future innovations in wearable technology are anticipated in the next decade?
9. **Ethical Considerations:** What ethical considerations arise when implementing technology that monitors personal health data?
10. **Motivation Effects:** Does the use of wearable technology actually motivate individuals to lead healthier lifestyles, or does it create pressure and anxiety?

Notes & Reflections

PART TWO
SOCIAL ORGANISATION

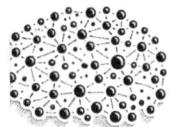

The arrangement of roles, relationships, and rules that structure how a society functions, influencing its cultural and social dynamics.

UNITY IN GROWTH

How do you think the concept of unity contributes to growth?

What kinds of collaborative or communal activities might be depicted in the image?

What impact do you believe growing together has on individuals and communities?

UNITY IN GROWTH

This image beautifully captures community members engaged in building a shared garden space in an urban neighborhood. The scene highlights the collective effort and cooperation among individuals of various ages and backgrounds, working together to create a sustainable and vibrant green space. The garden, nestled among city buildings, symbolizes the blending of urban living with environmental consciousness, emphasizing the importance of community-driven development and sustainable urban agriculture.

QUESTIONS FOR EXPLORATION

1. **Community Building:** How does participating in a community garden foster a sense of unity and belonging among diverse groups?
2. **Impact on Urban Aesthetics:** What impact do community gardens have on the aesthetic and environmental quality of urban neighborhoods?
3. **Social Benefits:** What are the social benefits of involving various cultural groups in community gardening projects?
4. **Sustainability Practices:** How can urban gardens contribute to sustainable urban living?
5. **Educational Opportunities:** What educational opportunities arise from community gardens for both children and adults?
6. **Food Security:** How do community gardens enhance food security in urban areas?
7. **Mental Health Benefits:** What are the therapeutic benefits that arise from community gardening and communal activities?
8. **Cultural Exchange:** How might community gardens serve as platforms for cultural exchange and understanding?
9. **Challenges and Barriers:** What are some common challenges or barriers to starting and maintaining community gardens in urban areas?
10. **Future of Urban Green Spaces:** What is the future role of community gardens in the development of smart and green cities?

UNITY IN GROWTH

Notes & Reflections

HARMONY IN CARE

What does the idea of harmony in caregiving or healthcare mean to you?

How might the image portray a harmonious environment?

What qualities or actions do you associate with creating a harmonious caregiving environment?

HARMONY IN CARE

This image portrays a group of seniors engaging with caregivers and family members in a high-tech assisted living facility. The setting is equipped with smart technologies like interactive displays and health monitoring devices that enhance communication and personalized care. The atmosphere is modern yet comforting, highlighting an environment that supports the well-being and independence of seniors.

QUESTIONS FOR EXPLORATION

1. **Technology in Elder Care:** How can smart technology transform the experience of living in assisted care facilities for seniors?
2. **Cultural Sensitivity:** How important is cultural sensitivity in the design and operation of senior living facilities?
3. **Family Engagement:** How does technology facilitate better engagement between seniors and their families?
4. **Privacy Concerns:** What are the potential privacy issues with the use of smart technologies in elder care?
5. **Training for Staff:** What type of training do caregivers need to effectively support a diverse group of elders?
6. **Cost Implications:** How does the integration of technology affect the cost of care in assisted living facilities?
7. **Health Monitoring:** How does continuous health monitoring change the care plans for seniors?
8. **Accessibility of Technology:** How accessible are these technologies for seniors with varying levels of tech-savviness?
9. **Impact on Independence:** Does technology in senior care enhance or diminish the sense of independence among the elderly?
10. **Future Trends:** What are the emerging trends in the use of technology in senior care facilities?

Notes and Reflections

BLUEPRINT FOR CHANGE

What elements do you think would be included in a blueprint designed for change?

How might the image depict the process or planning involved in creating change?

What areas of life or society do you imagine this blueprint addressing?

BLUEPRINT FOR CHANGE

This image captures a group of architects and local residents gathered around a blueprint in a public park, actively discussing plans to transform the area into a multifunctional community space. The setting is an existing urban park, with participants focused on integrating areas for various activities such as playgrounds, quiet zones, and sports facilities.

QUESTIONS FOR EXPLORATION

1. **Community Involvement:** How important is community involvement in the planning and redesign of public spaces?
2. **Functional Design:** What key elements should be considered to make urban parks more functional for different age groups and activities?
3. **Sustainability:** How can sustainability be integrated into the design of urban parks?
4. **Technology in Design:** What role does technology play in the planning and execution of urban park redesigns?
5. **Safety and Accessibility:** How can designers ensure that new park designs are safe and accessible to everyone, including those with disabilities?
6. **Economic Impact:** What are the potential economic impacts of redesigning urban parks on local communities?
7. **Social Cohesion:** How can the design of a park contribute to greater social cohesion within a community?
8. **Historical Preservation:** How can redesign efforts balance modern needs with the preservation of historical features in urban parks?
9. **Funding and Maintenance:** What are some effective strategies for funding and maintaining urban parks once they are upgraded?
10. **Long-term Benefits:** What are the long-term benefits of investing in well-designed urban parks for communities?

BLUEPRINT FOR CHANGE

Notes & Reflections

FESTIVAL FOUNDATIONS

What essential elements do you think are necessary to build the foundation of a festival?

How might the image capture the preparation and setup for a festival?

What cultural or personal significance do festivals hold, and how do you think this will be portrayed?

FESTIVAL FOUNDATIONS

This image captures a group of teenagers as they prepare a festival stall in an otherwise empty urban street. They are busy arranging colorful decorations and setting up merchandise, embodying the spirit of community involvement and youthful initiative. The setting highlights their contribution to the local festival, showcasing their role in bringing vibrancy and celebration to their community.

QUESTIONS FOR EXPLORATION

1. **Youth Engagement:** How important is it for teenagers to take active roles in community events?
2. **Impact on Skill Development:** What skills might the teenagers be learning through this experience?
3. **Cultural Significance:** How do festivals serve as a platform for cultural expression in urban environments?
4. **Community Building:** In what ways do such events strengthen community bonds?
5. **Economic Benefits:** What are the potential economic impacts of local festivals on small towns?
6. **Volunteerism:** How can communities encourage more youth to volunteer for local events?
7. **Environmental Considerations:** What environmental impacts should be considered when organizing street festivals?
8. **Safety Measures:** What safety measures are important for youth participating in public event preparations?
9. **Technological Integration:** Could technology enhance the organization and execution of such festivals?
10. **Future Participation:** What factors influence continued youth participation in community activities as they grow older?

FESTIVAL FOUNDATIONS

Notes & Reflections

URBAN TRANQUILITY

How do you imagine tranquility being achieved in an urban environment?

What elements or scenes do you expect to see that depict peace and calm within a bustling city?

What personal experiences or feelings do you associate with finding tranquility in a city setting?

URBAN TRANQUILITY

The image showcases an empty city street that highlights sustainable urban mobility. The scene is set against a backdrop of clear streets and modern architecture, devoid of any distractions, emphasizing the city's commitment to eco-friendly transportation solutions. This setting reflects an ideal urban environment that promotes the ease and accessibility of moving sustainably within a modern city.

QUESTIONS FOR EXPLORATION

1. **Urban Planning:** How does urban design influence the adoption of sustainable transportation methods?
2. **Youth Involvement:** What role do young people play in shaping the future of urban mobility?
3. **Architectural Impact:** How does architecture contribute to or hinder sustainable transportation in urban areas?
4. **Behavioral Changes:** What behavioral changes are necessary for individuals to adopt more sustainable transportation habits?
5. **Technology's Role:** How can technology enhance sustainable mobility in urban environments?
6. **Policy Incentives:** What policies could be implemented to encourage the use of sustainable transportation options?
7. **Environmental Benefits:** What are the key environmental benefits of promoting sustainable urban mobility?
8. **Social Influence:** What would urban transportation look like in your city? What would you propose?
9. **Future Trends:** What are the emerging trends in sustainable urban transportation?
10. **Cultural Shifts:** How do cultural perceptions of transportation need to change to embrace more sustainable practices?

URBAN TRANQUILITY

Notes & Reflections

RURAL REACH

What aspects of rural life do you think might be highlighted in the image?

How might the concept of "reach" be represented in a rural context?

What connections or contrasts between rural and urban areas do you imagine this title exploring?

RURAL REACH

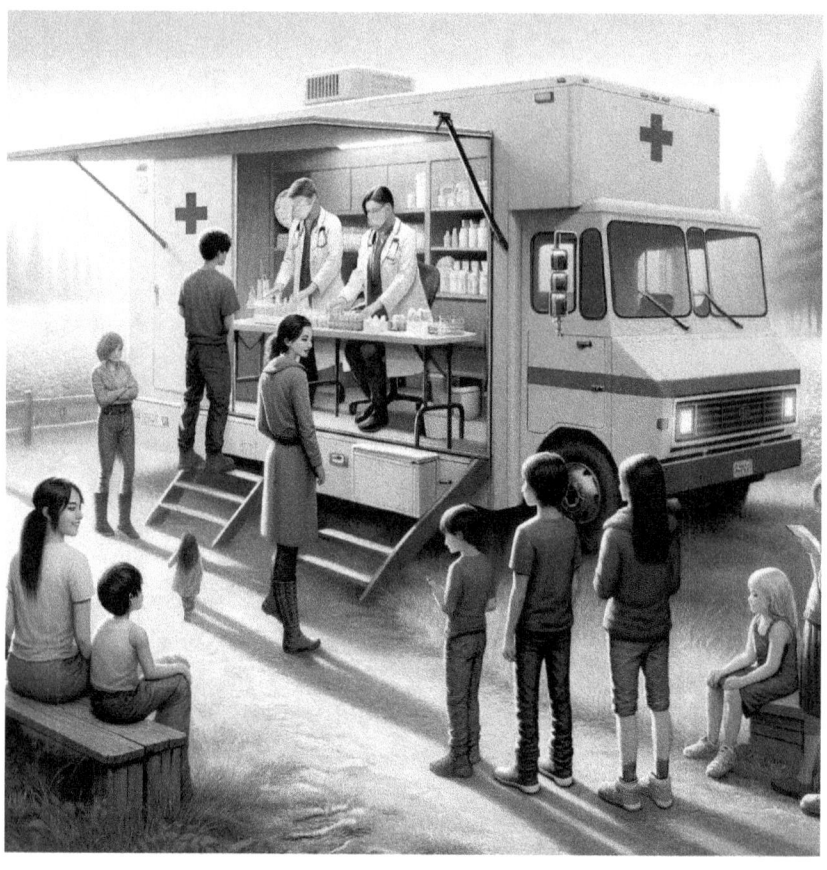

This image captures a scene at a mobile health clinic in a rural area, where young healthcare professionals, provide services to local patients. Wearing a surgical face mask, they symbolize the frontline efforts to enhance healthcare access in underserved regions. Set against the backdrop of nature and a mobile clinic unit, the image reflects the vital role of mobile healthcare services in rural communities.

QUESTIONS FOR EXPLORATION

1. **Healthcare Access**: How do mobile health clinics improve access to healthcare in rural areas?
2. **Community Impact**: What are the immediate and long-term impacts of mobile health clinics on rural communities?
3. **Challenges**: What challenges do mobile health clinics face in delivering services to remote areas?
4. **Technological Integration**: How can technology enhance the effectiveness of mobile health clinics?
5. **Global Healthcare Initiatives**: What strategies are countries around the world using to provide healthcare services in rural areas?
6. **Preventive Care**: How can mobile health clinics contribute to preventive care and health education in rural areas?
7. **Sustainability**: What strategies can ensure the sustainability of mobile health clinics?
8. **Collaborative Efforts**: How can local communities and organizations collaborate to support mobile health initiatives?
9. **Policy Support**: What policies are needed to support the expansion of mobile health services?
10. **Future Developments**: What future developments could improve the reach and impact of mobile health clinics in rural settings?

RURAL REACH

Notes & Reflections

EMPOWERING COMMUNITIES

What actions or initiatives do you think contribute to empowering communities?

How might the image depict the impact of community empowerment?

Have you ever been apart of an empowered community? What did it look and feel like?

EMPOWERING COMMUNITIES

This image showcases a neighborhood watch group training session in a vibrant urban setting, where community members and local law enforcement collaborate closely. This initiative reflects the community's commitment to improving safety through collective effort and proactive law enforcement engagement.

QUESTIONS FOR EXPLORATION

1. **Community Safety**: How do neighborhood watch programs contribute to the overall safety of a community?
2. **Trust Building**: What are effective ways to build trust between community members and local law enforcement?
3. **Participation**: How can communities encourage more residents to participate in neighborhood watch programs?
4. **Communication**: What communication strategies are vital for the success of a neighborhood watch program?
5. **Crime Prevention**: How do neighborhood watch programs help in preventing crime and enhancing security?
6. **Cultural Sensitivity**: Why is it important to consider cultural differences in neighborhood watch programs?
7. **Training**: What types of training are most beneficial for neighborhood watch participants?
8. **Resource Allocation**: How can communities ensure they have the necessary resources for an effective neighborhood watch?
9. **Technology Integration**: What role can technology play in modernizing neighborhood watch programs?
10. **Sustainability**: How can neighborhood watch programs be sustained over the long term?

EMPOWERING COMMUNITIES

Notes & Reflections

PREPARED TOGETHER

What situations or challenges do you think people might be preparing for together?

How might the image depict 'togetherness'?

What feelings or experiences do you associate with being prepared as a group?

PREPARED TOGETHER

This image vividly captures a community drill for natural disaster response in an urban setting. Residents alongside emergency personnel are seen coordinating rescue and relief efforts in a meticulously simulated disaster scenario.

QUESTIONS FOR EXPLORATION

1. **Community Preparedness:** How important is community involvement in disaster preparedness drills?
2. **Effectiveness of Drills:** What makes a disaster preparedness drill effective?
3. **Impact:** What are the benefits and drawbacks of participating in disaster drills for the community?
4. **Learning Outcomes:** What are the key lessons that residents typically learn from participating in these drills?
5. **Emergency Personnel Interaction:** How does regular interaction with emergency personnel during drills influence community trust and cooperation during actual disasters?
6. **Disaster Readiness:** How can communities improve their readiness for unexpected natural disasters?
7. **Youth Involvement:** What role do young people play in these drills, and how can their participation be enhanced?
8. **Technology and Drills:** How can technology be integrated into disaster preparedness drills to increase their effectiveness?
9. **Evaluation Methods:** What are the best methods to evaluate the effectiveness of disaster preparedness drills?
10. **Evolution of Disaster Response:** In what ways have countries improved their response to natural disasters by learning from past experiences?

Notes & Reflections

VOICES FOR CHANGE

What types of messages or causes do you think these voices are advocating for?

How might the image capture the power and impact of collective voices demanding change?

What emotions or movements do you associate with the idea of raising voices for change?

VOICES FOR CHANGE

This image captures a peaceful demonstration led by a group of teenagers in an urban environment, advocating for "Free Education For All." The scene is set in a bustling city square, where the commitment and unity of the young activists are palpable, showcasing their role in driving social change.

CHAPTERS FOR EXPLORATION

1. **Effectiveness of Message:** How effective is a message when banners are used in demonstrations?
2. **Digital Activism:** How has digital activism changed the way social movements organize and communicate?
3. **Youth Leadership:** What role do young people play in shaping policy discussions about education?
4. **Impact of Visuals:** How do visuals influence the public's reception of a protest's message?
5. **Community Support:** What factors influence community support for educational reforms promoted by youth?
6. **Legal Implications:** What are the legal considerations for youths organizing and participating in public demonstrations?
7. **Global Movement:** How can movements for educational reform benefit from international support and recognition?
8. **Educational Equity:** How does free education contribute to greater social and economic equity?
9. **Government Response:** How do governments typically respond to public demands for free education, and why?
10. **Long-term Outcomes:** What long-term outcomes can movements like these realistically aim to achieve?

VOICES FOR CHANGE

Notes & Reflections

URBAN OASIS

What do you envision an oasis in an urban environment to look like?

How might the image depict a place of peace and relaxation within a busy city?

Do you know of an urban oasis in your city or town? Describe it.

URBAN OASIS

This image captures a vibrant rooftop garden nestled among urban skyscrapers, where people of diverse ages and backgrounds engage in sustainable farming. This lush, green space atop a city building illustrates a successful integration of nature and urban life, serving as a beacon of community and environmental stewardship.

QUESTIONS FOR EXPLORATION

1. **Community Impact:** How do rooftop gardens contribute to community building in urban areas?
2. **Environmental Benefits:** What are the environmental benefits of integrating green spaces like rooftop gardens in densely populated cities?
3. **Food Security:** Can rooftop gardens significantly contribute to urban food security?
4. **Educational Opportunities:** What educational opportunities do rooftop gardens provide for urban residents, especially children?
5. **Biodiversity:** How can rooftop gardens help increase biodiversity in urban settings?
6. **Economic Viability:** What are the economic challenges and benefits of developing rooftop gardens in urban areas?
7. **Design Challenges:** What are some of the most significant design challenges when creating rooftop gardens on existing buildings?
8. **Policy Incentives:** What kind of policies could governments implement to encourage the creation of more rooftop gardens?
9. **Social Wellbeing:** How might access to green spaces like rooftop gardens affect the mental health and wellbeing of urban residents?
10. **Sustainability Practices**: What sustainable practices can be enhanced or introduced in rooftop gardening to promote eco-friendliness?

URBAN OASIS

Notes & Reflections

PART THREE
EXPERIENCES

Events and interactions that profoundly shape individuals' perceptions and decisions.

JOURNEY OF DISCOVERY

What kinds of adventures or explorations do you imagine on a journey of discovery?

How might the image depict the process of uncovering new knowledge or experiences?

What emotions or personal growth do you associate with embarking on a journey of discovery? Could you share one?

JOURNEY OF DISCOVERY

This image captures a young adult's transformative journey through a scenic mountain range in a foreign country. The character, is seen interacting with local villagers and learning traditional crafts, deeply immersed in cultural exchange. Set against the backdrop of lush green mountains and a rustic village, the scene portrays the essence of personal growth and cultural immersion during a gap year adventure.

QUESTIONS FOR EXPLORATION

1. **Cultural Exchange:** How can interactions with local communities during travels enhance understanding and appreciation of different cultures?
2. **Skills Acquisition:** What unique skills can one acquire through learning traditional crafts from local villagers?
3. **Impact on Locals:** How do travelers impact the local communities they visit, both positively and negatively?
4. **Sustainable Travel:** What practices can make such travel adventures more sustainable and ethical?
5. **Personal Growth:** In what ways can a gap year contribute to personal development and self-discovery?
6. **Economic Contributions:** How can travelers contribute economically to the communities they visit without causing disruption?
7. **Language Barriers:** What are the challenges and rewards of navigating language barriers during such trips?
8. **Preparation for Travels:** What preparations are essential for a successful gap year focused on cultural immersion?
9. **Long-Term Effects:** How might such an experience influence one's career path or life choices?
10. **Cultural Sensitivity:** How can travelers ensure they are being culturally sensitive and respectful during their adventures?

JOURNEY OF DISCOVERY

Notes & Reflections

NEW HORIZONS

What do you envision when you think of exploring new horizons?

How might the image capture the excitement and uncertainty of venturing into the unknown?

What personal or collective changes do you associate with discovering new horizons?

NEW HORIZONS

This image captures the first moments of a family as they step into a bustling airport, having just arrived in a new country. Clutching their modest collection of belongings, their faces are a canvas of mixed emotions. The bustling surroundings contrast sharply with their tentative steps, emphasizing the enormity of their journey and the resilience required to navigate this new chapter.

QUESTIONS FOR EXPLORATION

1. **Emotional Impact:** What emotional challenges might families face when moving to a new country?
2. **Cultural Adjustment:** How can families preserve their cultural identity while adapting to a new cultural environment?
3. **Support Systems:** What role do support systems play in helping immigrant families settle in new countries?
4. **Language Barriers:** How do language barriers affect the integration process for immigrant families?
5. **Education for Children:** What challenges do children from immigrant families face in new educational systems?
6. **Economic Opportunities:** How does migration affect the economic opportunities available to families?
7. **Policy Influence:** How can government policies ease the transition for immigrant families?
8. **Community Engagement:** How important is community engagement in the successful integration of immigrant families?
9. **Mental Health:** What mental health resources are essential for families adjusting to a new life in a different country?
10. **Long-term Outcomes:** What are the long-term outcomes for families that migrate to new countries in terms of cultural integration and quality of life?

NEW HORIZONS

Notes & Reflections

THE FINAL STRETCH

What feelings or thoughts come to mind when you think of the final stretch of a journey or project?

How might the image depict the determination and effort involved in completing something important?

What experiences or challenges do you associate with reaching the final stretch?

THE FINAL STRETCH

This image captures the moment an athlete crosses the finish line of a marathon, displaying a vivid expression of both exhaustion and elation. Surrounded by an enthusiastic crowd, the scene highlights the intense emotional highs and lows experienced by athletes in competitive sports.

QUESTIONS FOR EXPLORATION

1. **Psychological Impact:** How do athletes prepare mentally for the psychological challenges of a marathon?
2. **Physical Training:** What are key physical training techniques that help athletes endure long-distance races?
3. **Crowd Influence:** How does the presence of a cheering crowd affect an athlete's performance in the final moments of a race?
4. **Recovery Strategies:** What are effective recovery strategies after completing a marathon?
5. **Motivation:** What motivates individuals to participate in physically demanding events like marathons?
6. **Personal Stories:** What are some inspiring stories of personal triumph you know from ultimate athletes?
7. **Impact of Weather:** How can adverse weather conditions affect the outcome of a marathon?
8. **Sponsorship and Support:** What role do sponsorships play in supporting elite and amateur athletes?
9. **Community and Connection:** How do marathons contribute to building community and connections among participants?
10. **Future Aspirations:** After completing an event, what future goals do athletes typically set for themselves?

THE FINAL STRETCH

Notes & Reflections

REALM OF SILENCE

What emotions or sensations do you associate with a realm of silence?

How do you imagine the image capturing the essence of silence in a particular setting?

What stories or reflections do you think could emerge from a place characterized by silence?

REALM OF SILENCE

This image presents a darker, more realistic view of an international space station orbiting Earth. Astronauts of diverse backgrounds conduct zero-gravity experiments, visible through large panoramic windows that frame the breathtaking curvature of Earth. This portrayal emphasizes the isolation and the significant responsibilities faced by those on the forefront of space exploration.

QUESTIONS FOR EXPLORATION

1. **Realism in Space Depictions:** How does a more realistic portrayal of space environments, like in this image, affect our understanding and appreciation of astronaut experiences?
2. **Cultural Representation:** What is the importance of having a diverse crew in space missions? How does it impact team dynamics and problem-solving?
3. **Psychological Effects:** What psychological challenges might astronauts face in such an isolated and high-stakes environment?
4. **Technology Reliance:** Considering the advanced technology depicted, how reliant are astronauts on these tools, and what happens if they fail?
5. **Scientific Research:** What types of experiments might the crew be conducting, and how could these benefit humanity?
6. **Communication with Earth:** How do astronauts communicate their findings and challenges back to Earth, and what are the implications of any delays in communication?
7. **Design Considerations:** What design elements are crucial for the functionality and safety of space stations, as seen in this image?
8. **Sustainability in Space:** How are resources managed sustainably on a space station?
9. **Ethical Questions:** What ethical considerations arise when sending humans on long-duration space missions?
10. **Future of Space Stations:** What does the future hold for international collaborations in space exploration?

REALM OF SILENCE

Notes & Reflections

TOMORROW'S CLASSROOM

WHAT TECHNOLOGICAL OR EDUCATIONAL ADVANCEMENTS DO YOU ENVISION IN A FUTURE CLASSROOM?

HOW MIGHT THE IMAGE DEPICT THE INTERACTIONS AND LEARNING EXPERIENCES IN TOMORROW'S CLASSROOM?

WHAT CHANGES IN TEACHING AND LEARNING METHODS DO YOU THINK WILL SHAPE THE CLASSROOMS OF THE FUTURE?

TOMORROW'S CLASSROOM

This image showcases a modern classroom where a robot teacher engages a diverse group of young students. The classroom is bright and inviting, filled with natural light and colorful educational materials. The robot, sleek and friendly, stands in front of a smart blackboard that displays interactive AI-generated content, capturing the students' attention and curiosity.

QUESTIONS FOR EXPLORATION

1. **Educational Impact:** How might AI-enhanced teaching methods improve learning outcomes for students of various backgrounds?
2. **Teacher Role:** What is the role of human teachers when AI can deliver personalized learning experiences?
3. **Engagement Levels:** How does the use of AI in the classroom affect student engagement and interest in learning?
4. **Ethical Considerations:** What are the ethical implications of using AI to teach children, especially in terms of privacy and data security?
5. **Accessibility:** How can AI teaching tools be made accessible to schools in underprivileged or remote areas?
6. **Cultural Sensitivity:** How can AI systems be designed to be culturally sensitive and inclusive to all students?
7. **Skill Development:** What types of new skills do students need to learn to effectively interact with AI in their education?
8. **Parental Perspective:** How do parents view the integration of AI into their children's education?
9. **Future Classrooms:** What might the classroom of the future look like if AI continues to advance and integrate into education?
10. **Digital Divide:** How can educators ensure that the digital divide does not widen as AI becomes more prevalent in schools?

TOMORROW'S CLASSROOM

Notes & Reflections

CROSSING CULTURES

What do you imagine when you think about the experience of crossing cultures?

How might the image depict the blending or interaction of different cultural elements?

What personal or societal transformations do you associate with the exchange of cultural ideas and practices?

CROSSING CULTURES

This image illustrates the journey of a student participating in a study exchange, exploring ancient ruins and engaging with local scholars. This scene highlights the educational depth and interpersonal exchanges that shape such culturally rich experiences, offering insights into both the complexities and rewards of learning in an international context.

QUESTIONS FOR EXPLORATION

1. **Cultural Adaptation:** What are some common challenges students face when adapting to a new cultural environment during a study exchange?
2. **Language Barriers:** How do language differences impact the learning and integration process in a study exchange program?
3. **Cultural Insights:** What unique insights do students gain from studying in culturally rich settings like ancient Greece?
4. **Interpersonal Relations:** How do interactions with local students and scholars enrich the study exchange experience?
5. **Overcoming Challenges:** What strategies can students employ to overcome cultural and academic challenges while abroad?
6. **Benefits of Exchange:** How does living and studying in a foreign country enhance a student's educational and personal development?
7. **Preparation Tips:** What preparation should students undertake to maximize their learning experience during study exchanges?
8. **Cultural Sensitivity:** How can students practice cultural sensitivity while participating in study exchange programs?
9. **Long-term Impact:** How might a study exchange influence a student's future academic and career choices?
10. **Sharing Experiences:** What are effective ways for students to share their study exchange experiences with their home institutions?

CROSSING CULTURES

Notes & Reflections

CITY SERENADES

What kinds of sounds or music do you associate with a city serenade?

How might the image capture the essence of a city's rhythm and melody?

What emotions or memories come to mind when you think of music?

CITY SERENADES

This image vividly captures a jazz musician playing a saxophone on a bustling city street at night, surrounded by captivated pedestrians. As the notes float through the air, they draw a diverse crowd, creating an impromptu concert under the city lights. The scene highlights the powerful connection between the musician and his audience, illustrating the profound impact of street performances on urban culture.

QUESTIONS FOR EXPLORATION

1. **Emotional Connection:** How does live music on the streets create an emotional connection between the musician and the audience?
2. **Cultural Influence:** What role does street performance play in shaping the cultural identity of a city?
3. **Community Building:** How can music contribute to community building in urban environments?
4. **Inspiration Sources:** Where do musicians find inspiration for their street performances?
5. **Public Space Usage:** How does the use of public spaces for performances influence people's perceptions of those areas?
6. **Artistic Expression:** What challenges do musicians face when expressing themselves in uncontrolled public environments?
7. **Audience Impact:** How does an impromptu audience affect the performance of a musician?
8. **Cultural Diversity:** How do street performances reflect the cultural diversity of a city?
9. **Economic Aspects:** Can street performances be economically sustainable for musicians?
10. **Technology and Music:** How has technology changed the way street performances are conducted and received by the public?

CITY SERENADES

Notes & Reflections

CANVAS OF LIGHT

What scenes or images do you imagine when you think of the title?

How might the image depict the interplay between light and art?

What feelings or stories do you associate with the idea of creating art?

CANVAS OF LIGHT

This image captures an artist immersed in the creative process within a bright, sunlit studio. Surrounded by an array of colorful art pieces, brushes, and open paint containers, the artist focuses intently on a large canvas. The studio, bathed in natural light, enhances the vivid colors of the artwork, creating an atmosphere of intense concentration and artistic freedom.

QUESTIONS FOR EXPLORATION

1. **Creative Environment:** How does the physical environment influence an artist's creativity?
2. **Artistic Process:** What stages does an artist go through when creating a new piece of art?
3. **Color Use:** How does the artist in the image use color to express emotions or ideas?
4. **Daily Rituals:** What daily rituals might help an artist stay focused and productive in their studio?
5. **Inspirational Sources:** From where do artists typically draw inspiration for their works?
6. **Material Choice:** How do different materials (paints, brushes, canvases) affect the outcome of artwork?
7. **Artistic Freedom:** What does artistic freedom mean, and how can it be seen in the artist's work?
8. **Emotional Connection:** How do artists embed personal experiences or emotions into their artworks?
9. **Public vs. Private Art:** How does creating art for a public audience differ from creating art for personal satisfaction?
10. **Evolution of Style:** How does an artist's style evolve over time, and what factors might influence this evolution?

CANVAS OF LIGHT

Notes & Reflections

FOREST SERENITY

What sights, sounds, or sensations do you imagine when you think of a forest?

How might the image depict the peaceful and calming aspects of a forest environment?

What personal experiences or feelings do you associate with finding tranquility in nature?

FOREST SERENITY

This image captures a profound moment of spiritual renewal with five individuals deeply immersed in a meditation session within a serene, lush green forest. The participants are seated in a circle, each engaged in a personal journey of inner peace, surrounded by towering trees and soft sunlight. This setting embodies tranquility and the harmonious connection between humans and nature.

QUESTIONS FOR EXPLORATION

1. **Impact of Environment:** How does the natural setting enhance the meditation experience?
2. **Personal Growth:** What personal transformations are often experienced during such spiritual retreats?
3. **Group Dynamics:** How does meditating in a group compare to meditating alone in terms of benefits and challenges?
4. **Spiritual Connection:** In what ways can a spiritual retreat deepen one's connection with nature?
5. **Accessibility:** What are some ways to make spiritual retreats more accessible to people from different walks of life?
6. **Mindfulness Techniques:** What mindfulness techniques can be particularly effective when practiced in natural settings?
7. **Stress Reduction:** How do retreats like these impact stress and overall well-being?
8. **Cultural Practices:** How do different cultures incorporate nature into their spiritual or meditative practices?
9. **Sustainability:** What considerations should be taken to ensure such retreats are sustainable and minimize impact on the environment?
10. **Future Retreats:** What trends or new approaches are emerging in the planning and execution of spiritual retreats?

FOREST SERENITY

Notes & Reflections

TIME TO RELAX

What activities or settings do you envision when you think about taking time to relax?

How might the image capture the essence of relaxation and unwinding?

What emotions or experiences do you associate with finding a moment of peace and relaxation?

TIME TO RELAX

This image showcases four young teens engaged in their favorite leisure activities in a lush, outdoor park setting. This scene captures the essence of individuality and the importance of leisure time in the personal growth and relaxation of young people.

QUESTIONS FOR EXPLORATION

1. **Cultural Significance:** How do leisure activities reflect cultural backgrounds and personal identities?
2. **Impact on Development:** What role do leisure activities play in the cognitive and social development of teenagers?
3. **Balance in Life:** How important is it for young people to balance their educational and leisure activities?
4. **Technology Influence:** In what ways has technology shaped the leisure activities that today's youth engage in?
5. **Outdoor vs. Indoor:** How do outdoor leisure activities compare to indoor ones in terms of benefits to young people?
6. **Accessibility:** Are leisure activities equally accessible to all youth regardless of their socioeconomic background?
7. **Influence on Relationships:** How do leisure activities influence friendships and social interactions among teens?
8. **Changes Over Time:** How have common leisure activities for teens changed over the past few decades?
9. **Parental Perspective:** What concerns might parents have about their children's leisure activities, and how can they effectively communicate about these?
10. **Future Trends:** What future trends might emerge in the leisure activities of young people?

TIME TO RELAX

Notes & Reflections

PART FOUR
SHARING THE PLANET

The concept of coexistence and mutual responsibility among all living beings on Earth.

FLOW OF THE FUTURE

What advancements or innovations do you think will shape the future?

How might the image depict the seamless integration of technology and daily life?

What emotions or visions do you associate with the continuous progress and flow towards the future?

This Image showcases a bustling city intersection where autonomous electric vehicles, bicycles, and pedestrians coexist seamlessly. Managed by a smart traffic control system, the intersection exemplifies efficiency and safety, with clear markings for dedicated lanes and state-of-the-art traffic management technologies.

QUESTIONS FOR EXPLORATION

1. **Urban Planning:** How does smart traffic control technology impact urban planning and city living?
2. **Safety Improvements:** In what ways do autonomous vehicles and smart traffic systems enhance safety for all road users?
3. **Environmental Impact:** How can the integration of autonomous vehicles and smart systems at city intersections contribute to environmental sustainability?
4. **Data Privacy:** What privacy concerns might arise with the widespread use of smart traffic systems that monitor and control flow?
5. **Public Acceptance:** How can cities encourage public acceptance and trust in autonomous vehicles and smart traffic technologies?
6. **Economic Factors:** What are the economic benefits and challenges of implementing smart traffic systems in urban areas?
7. **Infrastructure Changes:** What infrastructure modifications are necessary to accommodate smart traffic systems and autonomous vehicles?
8. **Impact on Traffic Congestion:** How effective are smart traffic systems in reducing traffic congestion compared to traditional methods?
9. **Accessibility and Inclusion:** How do smart traffic systems address the needs of all citizens, including those with disabilities?
10. **Future Trends:** What are the potential future developments in smart traffic technology, and how might they further transform urban areas?

FLOW OF THE FUTURE

Notes & Reflections

SEEDS OF RENEWAL

WHAT IMAGES OR SYMBOLS DO YOU ASSOCIATE WITH THE IDEA OF RENEWAL AND NEW BEGINNINGS?

HOW MIGHT THE IMAGE DEPICT THE GROWTH AND TRANSFORMATION THAT COMES FROM PLANTING SEEDS?

WHAT PERSONAL OR COLLECTIVE CHANGES DO YOU THINK ARE SPARKED BY THE CONCEPT OF RENEWAL?

SEEDS OF RENEWAL

This image captures a critical moment of ecological restoration, where drones fly over a stark, deforested landscape, systematically dropping seed pods. The technology-driven reforestation effort is coordinated by a control team from a mobile command center, equipped with advanced monitoring systems.

QUESTIONS FOR EXPLORATION

1. **Efficiency and Effectiveness:** How effective are drones compared to traditional reforestation methods in terms of speed, coverage, and survival rates of seedlings?
2. **Technological Integration:** What technological advancements make drone-based reforestation possible, and how can these technologies be improved?
3. **Environmental Impact:** What are the immediate and long-term environmental impacts of using drones for reforestation?
4. **Economic Viability:** How economically viable is drone reforestation for large-scale projects in diverse geographic locations?
5. **Biodiversity Considerations:** How can drones be used to ensure biodiversity is considered and preserved during reforestation efforts?
6. **Community Involvement:** What role can local communities play in drone-assisted reforestation projects?
7. **Regulatory Challenges:** What are the regulatory implications and challenges of using drones for environmental restoration?
8. **Data Accuracy:** How accurate are the data collected by drones, and how does this influence reforestation strategies?
9. **Scalability Issues:** What are the scalability issues associated with drone reforestation, and how can they be addressed?
10. **Future Prospects:** What future developments can be anticipated in the field of drone technology for environmental restoration?

Notes & Reflections

TIDES OF CHANGE

What do you imagine when you think about the power and movement of tides representing change?

How might the image depict the dynamic and sometimes unpredictable nature of change?

What personal or societal transformations do you associate with the concept of changing tides?

TIDES OF CHANGE

This image portrays a distressing yet urgent scene at a beach, where the shore is littered with plastic waste, and seabirds are seen navigating through the pollution. The depiction serves as a stark reminder of the severe impact that human activities, particularly plastic waste, have on marine environments and wildlife. The visual emphasizes the pressing need for collective action and greater environmental awareness to address this escalating crisis.

QUESTIONS FOR EXPLORATION

1. **Awareness and Impact:** How does seeing images of pollution affect public perception and behavior towards plastic use?
2. **Wildlife Conservation:** What are the immediate and long-term effects of plastic pollution on marine wildlife?
3. **Community Actions:** What community-led initiatives can be effective in combating beach and ocean pollution?
4. **Policy Solutions:** What policies could governments implement to reduce the production and consumption of single-use plastics?
5. **Recycling and Alternatives:** How effective is recycling in mitigating plastic pollution, and what alternatives to plastic are most promising?
6. **Global Cooperation:** How important is international cooperation in addressing the issue of marine plastic pollution?
7. **Educational Initiatives:** What role can education play in shaping a more environmentally conscious future generation?
8. **Corporate Responsibility:** What responsibility do corporations have in reducing their plastic footprint?
9. **Personal Choices:** How can individual choices and actions make a difference in reducing plastic pollution?
10. **Technological Innovations:** What are some technological innovations that could help clean up existing pollution and prevent future contamination?

TIDES OF CHANGE

Notes & Reflections

GUARDIANS OF GREEN

What do you envision when you think about individuals or groups acting as protectors of nature?

How might the image depict the dedication and actions of those who work to preserve the environment?

What stories can you share about how you have been a guardian of the natural world?

GUARDIANS OF GREEN

This image captures a solitary conservationist meticulously setting up monitoring devices in a dense bamboo forest. With his back to the camera, the focus is on his interaction with the lush surroundings, emphasizing his role in environmental protection and wildlife conservation. The photorealistic depiction highlights the immersive experience of working in the heart of nature, underscoring the dedication required to sustain these vital ecosystems.

QUESTIONS FOR EXPLORATION

1. **Conservation Technology:** How does technology enhance our ability to monitor and protect wildlife?
2. **Role of Conservationists:** What challenges do conservationists face when working in remote and dense environments?
3. **Impact on Wildlife:** How might the presence of monitoring equipment affect the natural behavior of wildlife?
4. **Data Usage:** What kind of data is most crucial for conservation efforts, and how can it be used to make a significant impact?
5. **Funding and Resources:** How are conservation projects like these funded, and what resources are most critical for their success?
6. **Local vs. Global Efforts:** How do local conservation efforts contribute to global environmental goals?
7. **Ethical Considerations:** What ethical considerations must be taken into account when intervening in natural habitats?
8. **Education and Awareness:** How can the general public be educated through the findings from such conservation efforts?
9. **Career Paths:** What pathways exist for someone interested in becoming a conservationist?
10. **Future Technologies:** What emerging technologies hold promise for the future of wildlife conservation?

Notes & Reflections

VOICES OF SILENCE

What messages or stories do you think are conveyed through silence?

How might the image capture the contrast between sound and silence?

What emotions or reflections do you associate with the concept of silent voices?

VOICES OF SILENCE

This image captures a peaceful protest in an urban setting, where people of various backgrounds are sitting on the ground with their faces covered, symbolizing unity and the fight for equality. The protesters, each with a mask or cloth covering their face, are shown sitting in solidarity on a city street.

QUESTIONS FOR EXPLORATION

1. **Visual Impact:** How does the act of covering faces impact the message of the protest?
2. **Unity Definition:** What does unity mean in the context of diverse backgrounds coming together for a common cause?
3. **Influence on Perception:** How can peaceful protests influence public perception and policy?
4. **Organizational Challenges:** What are the challenges of organizing a peaceful protest in urban areas?
5. **Dialogue Shaping:** How do such protests shape the dialogue around social justice?
6. **Location Symbolism:** What role does location play in the symbolism and effectiveness of a protest?
7. **Cultural Interpretations:** How do different cultures interpret the symbolism of masked protests?
8. **Safety Considerations:** What safety considerations are important during such public demonstrations?
9. **Digital Age Effects:** How has the digital age affected the organization and impact of peaceful protests?
10. **Historical Comparisons:** What historical protests can be compared to this scene in terms of impact and methods?

Notes & Reflections

GREEN IN THE CITY

What types of green spaces or elements do you imagine being integrated into an urban environment?

How might the image depict the coexistence of nature and city life?

What benefits or challenges do you associate with bringing more greenery into urban areas?

GREEN IN THE CITY

This image showcases a bustling city park, a vibrant hub of activity and tranquility in the heart of a dense urban area. Surrounded by towering buildings, the park serves as a vital green space where people of all ages and backgrounds come together. Children play energetically on playground equipment while adults relax and socialize, highlighting the park's role as both a community gathering spot and a personal retreat from the urban environment.

QUESTIONS FOR EXPLORATION

1. **Urban Planning:** How do green spaces like city parks contribute to urban planning and the quality of life in metropolitan areas?
2. **Community Impact:** What role do parks play in fostering community interaction and cohesion?
3. **Environmental Benefits:** What are the environmental benefits of incorporating green spaces in urban areas?
4. **Mental Health:** How do urban parks affect the mental health of city dwellers?
5. **Accessibility:** How accessible are green spaces in your city, and what improvements could be made?
6. **Design and Maintenance:** What features should be included in the design of urban parks to maximize their use and enjoyment?
7. **Cultural Events:** ow can urban parks be used to promote cultural activities and events?
8. **Safety:** What measures can be taken to ensure safety in urban parks?
9. **Sustainability:** How can sustainability be integrated into the development and upkeep of urban parks?
10. **Future Trends:** What trends are emerging in the design and use of urban parks in major cities worldwide?

… GREEN IN THE CITY

Notes & Reflections

HORIZONS OF HOPE

WHAT IMAGES OR SCENES DO YOU ENVISION WHEN YOU THINK ABOUT NEW HORIZONS FILLED WITH HOPE?

HOW MIGHT THE IMAGE CAPTURE THE FEELINGS OF OPTIMISM AND POTENTIAL FOR THE FUTURE?

WHAT PERSONAL OR COLLECTIVE ASPIRATIONS DO YOU ASSOCIATE WITH THE IDEA OF HOPEFUL HORIZONS?

HORIZONS OF HOPE

This image captures a breathtaking sunset at a wind farm, where multiple turbines spin steadily, a family nearby watching in awe. The scene symbolizes the community's growing commitment to renewable energy sources, with the wind farm serving as a powerful representation of sustainable progress.

QUESTIONS FOR EXPLORATION

1. **Visual Impact:** How does the visual impact of wind farms in natural settings affect public perception of renewable energy?
2. **Energy Benefits:** What are the primary benefits of wind energy compared to other renewable energy sources?
3. **Community Involvement:** How can communities be involved in the development and benefits of local renewable energy projects?
4. **Integration Challenges:** What are the challenges of integrating wind farms into existing landscapes and ecosystems?
5. **Sustainable Goals:** How does wind energy contribute to the goals of sustainable development?
6. **Technological Advancements:** What technological advancements are on the horizon for wind energy?
7. **Role of Education:** How can education play a role in increasing acceptance and support for wind energy?
8. **Government Policies:** What policies can governments implement to encourage the adoption of wind energy?
9. **Economic Impact:** How do wind farms like this one impact the local economy and job market?
10. **Environmental Impacts:** What are the long-term environmental impacts of wind farms on their surrounding areas?

Notes & Reflections

DESERT INNOVATION

What types of innovative solutions do you think might be developed to thrive in a desert environment?

How might the image depict the blending of technology and nature in a desert setting?

What challenges and opportunities do you associate with creating advancements in such an extreme landscape?

DESERT INNOVATION

This image showcases a community in a desert region actively implementing water-saving technologies like drip irrigation and water recycling. It captures the essence of resilience and sustainability as residents and farmers manage water resources efficiently amid arid conditions. The scene highlights advanced irrigation systems and water recycling methods that are crucial for adapting to the harsh desert environment, demonstrating the community's commitment to sustainable agriculture and daily water usage.

QUESTIONS FOR EXPLORATION

1. **Adaptation Strategies:** How do communities in desert regions adapt their water usage to overcome scarcity?
2. **Technology Impact:** What impact do modern water-saving technologies have on agricultural productivity in arid areas?
3. **Economic Benefits:** How do water conservation practices affect the economic stability of desert communities?
4. **Cultural Shifts:** What cultural shifts are necessary for the adoption of new water-saving technologies?
5. **Environmental Effects:** How do water conservation techniques impact the local desert ecosystem?
6. **Global Lessons:** What other irrigation systems have had a profound impact on local and international environments? **Policy Support:** What policies are essential to support water conservation efforts in desert areas?
7. **Community Engagement:** How important is community engagement in the success of water conservation initiatives?
8. **Technological Challenges:** What are the main challenges faced when implementing these technologies in remote or rural areas?
9. **Future Technologies:** What future technologies hold promise for improving water conservation in desert environments?

DESERT INNOVATION

Notes & Reflections

PLASTIC SHELLS

What environmental or societal issues do you think are highlighted by the concept of plastic shells?

How might the image depict the impact of plastic pollution on marine life?

Can you share a time where you have helped support animals in need?

PLASTIC SHELLS

This striking image portrays a group of turtles swimming in the ocean, their shells eerily replaced by plastic bags. This surreal visual serves as a poignant commentary on the devastating impact of plastic pollution in marine environments.

QUESTIONS FOR EXPLORATION

1. **Visual Symbolism**: How does the imagery of turtles with plastic bag shells impact your perception of ocean pollution?
2. **Artistic Expression**: In what ways does using plastic bags as turtle shells serve as a powerful metaphor for environmental degradation?
3. **Emotional Impact**: How does the surreal nature of the image evoke an emotional response from the viewer?
4. **Awareness Tools**: How can art like this image be used effectively to raise awareness about environmental issues?
5. **Creative Messaging**: What other symbols could be used to depict the effects of pollution on wildlife?
6. **Contrast and Clarity**: How does the contrast between the natural environment and the plastic bags enhance the message of the image?
7. **Engagement**: How might this image engage different audiences in discussions about pollution and conservation?
8. **Personal Reflection**: What personal actions or changes might someone consider after viewing this image?
9. **Cultural Influence**: How can cultural and artistic representations influence public opinion and policy on environmental issues?
10. **Local Awareness**: What particular issue in your location would you like to raise awareness about, and how would your image look?

PLASTIC SHELLS

Notes & Reflections

REVERSED REALITIES

What do you envision when you think about realities being reversed or flipped upside down?

How might the image portray the juxtaposition of familiar and unfamiliar elements in a reversed reality?

What emotions or thoughts do you associate with the concept of experiencing life from an entirely different perspective?

REVERSED REALITIES

This image presents a stark and surreal depiction of role reversal, where a cow walks freely past humans confined in battery farm cages, their faces obscured by masks. Set in an industrial environment, the scene is designed to provoke thought and stir debate on the ethics of animal farming.

QUESTIONS FOR EXPLORATION

1. **Emotional Response:** What emotions does this role reversal provoke, and why?
2. **Symbolic Masks:** How have brands used animals in advertisements to convey a product's message or vision? Can you share relevant examples?
3. **Ethical Queries:** What ethical questions does this scene raise about our current farming practices?
4. **Perspective Challenge:** In what ways does this image challenge your views on animal rights and human consumption?
5. **Communication Through Art:** How does the visual representation of role reversal help communicate the plight of animals in farms?
6. **Art and Social Change:** Can art be an effective tool for social change in issues like animal rights?
7. **Animal Treatment:** What are the implications of treating animals as products rather than sentient beings?
8. **Consumer Influence:** How might this image influence consumer behavior towards animal products?
9. **Promoting Ethics:** What steps can individuals take to promote more ethical treatment of animals?
10. **Legislative Solutions:** What role can legislation play in protecting animal welfare in the agricultural industry?

REVERSED REALITIES

Notes & Reflections

PART FIVE
IDENTITIES

The diverse aspects that define individuals and groups, including culture, ethnicity, gender, and beliefs, shaping how we see ourselves and how others perceive us.

BEFORE THE CHORDS

What do you imagine happens in the moments leading up to the first chords of a piece of music?

How might the image capture the power of music and Identity?

What emotions or experiences do you associate with the prelude to a musical performance?

BEFORE THE CHORDS

This image vividly captures four punks sitting outside a music venue, each adorned in iconic punk fashion from spiked hair to leather jackets, as they wait to enter. The setting, featuring the gritty exterior of the venue complete with posters and graffiti, perfectly encapsulates the rebellious and urban vibe of the punk scene.

QUESTIONS FOR EXPLORATION

1. **Cultural Statement:** What does punk fashion communicate about the cultural and social statements of the punk scene?
2. **Venue Influence:** How does the setting of a music venue contribute to the identity and atmosphere of punk music?
3. **Community Belonging:** In what ways do punk communities foster a sense of belonging among their members?
4. **Musical Influence:** How has punk music influenced broader music genres and cultural movements?
5. **Defining Elements:** What are the key elements that define punk music and its subculture?
6. **Aesthetic Challenges:** How do punk aesthetics challenge conventional norms and expectations?
7. **Role of Camaraderie:** What role does camaraderie play in the survival and evolution of punk culture?
8. **Digital Impact:** How has the digital age affected the traditional punk scene and its community gatherings?
9. **Lessons in Rebellion:** What can be learned about rebellion and resistance from punk culture?
10. **Cultural Reflection:** How does punk music and its culture reflect the political and social anxieties of its time?

BEFORE THE CHORDS

Notes & Reflections

SYMPHONY OF CULTURES

How do you envision different cultures coming together to create a harmonious symphony?

What elements or scenes might the image depict to show the blend and celebration of diverse cultural traditions?

What emotions or reflections do you associate with the experience of different cultures interacting and enriching each other?

SYMPHONY OF CULTURES

This image captures a vibrant scene of musicians from diverse cultural backgrounds collaborating in a studio. Surrounded by a mix of traditional and modern instruments—from sitars and djembes to electric guitars and synthesizers—each musician contributes their unique sound, creating a rich tapestry of musical fusion.

QUESTIONS FOR EXPLORATION

1. **Instrumental Fusion:** How does the blend of traditional and modern instruments enhance the music created?
2. **Collaborative Challenges:** What challenges might arise when musicians from different cultural backgrounds collaborate?
3. **Music as a Bridge:** How can music act as a universal language to bridge cultural divides?
4. **Benefits of Diversity:** What are the benefits of incorporating diverse musical styles into new compositions?
5. **Cultural Influence:** How does each musician's cultural heritage influence their approach to music?
6. **Cultural Identity:** What role does music play in maintaining cultural identity in a globalized world?
7. **Mutual Understanding:** How can collaborative music projects promote mutual understanding and respect among cultures?
8. **Global Impact:** What impact can such fusion music have on the global music scene?
9. **Audience Perception:** How do audiences perceive and receive music that blends multiple cultural elements?
10. **Future Collaborations:** What future possibilities exist for cross-cultural musical collaborations?

SYMPHONY OF CULTURES

Notes & Reflections

EXTREME EXPERIENCES

What kinds of activities or situations do you envision when you think of extreme experiences?

How might the image capture the intensity and thrill of pushing physical or mental limits?

What emotions or personal growth do you associate with participating in or witnessing extreme experiences?

EXTREME EXPERIENCES

This image vividly captures the essence of youth culture in an urban skate park, where teenagers engage in skateboarding and graffiti art. The park buzzes with the energy of young skaters performing daring tricks, while others channel their artistic flair into vibrant graffiti on the park's walls.

QUESTIONS FOR EXPLORATION

1. **Expression of Identity:** How do skateboarding and graffiti serve as forms of self-expression for teenagers?
2. **Impact on Public Spaces:** What impact do youth subcultures like skateboarding and graffiti have on public spaces?
3. **Perception of Graffiti:** How has the public perception of graffiti changed over the years?
4. **Influence of Subcultures:** How do youth subcultures influence fashion, music, and art in broader culture?
5. **Safety and Regulation:** What safety measures and regulations should be considered in skate parks?
6. **Legal Implications:** What are the legal implications of graffiti as an art form in public spaces?
7. **Community Building:** How do activities like skateboarding and graffiti art foster community among youth?
8. **Access to Public Spaces:** How accessible are public spaces like skate parks to all teenagers?
9. **Cultural Diversity:** How do these subcultures bring together teenagers from different cultural backgrounds?
10. **Future of Urban Youth Culture:** What is the future of urban youth cultures like skateboarding and graffiti art in the digital age?

EXTREME EXPERIENCES

Notes & Reflections

SCREENS OF SELF

How do you think digital screens influence our understanding and expression of self-identity?

What might the image depict to show the relationship between technology and personal reflection?

What emotions or thoughts do you associate with the idea of viewing oneself through the lens of a screen?

SCREENS OF SELF

This image captures a teenager in their room, immersed in a digital environment with multiple screens displaying various facets of their digital life, including social media profiles, video games, and virtual reality gear. The room highlights the profound impact of digital worlds on personal identity.

QUESTIONS FOR EXPLORATION

1. **Identity Formation:** How do digital platforms influence the formation of personal identity among teenagers?
2. **Social Interaction:** What role do social media and online games play in shaping social interactions for today's youth?
3. **Privacy Concerns:** What are the privacy implications of having a prominent digital presence?
4. **Mental Health:** How can prolonged exposure to digital screens impact mental health?
5. **Educational Impact:** What educational benefits and drawbacks come with the integration of digital tools in learning environments?
6. **Reality Perception:** How does virtual reality affect a teenager's perception of reality and social norms?
7. **Content Creation:** How does the ability to create and share content online empower or pressure teenagers?
8. **Parental Guidance:** What role should parents play in managing or overseeing their children's digital engagements?
9. **Digital Etiquette:** How important is digital etiquette, and how can it be taught effectively?
10. **Future Trends:** What future developments in digital technology could further impact youth identity formation?

SCREENS OF SELF

Notes & Reflections

CANVAS OF COMMUNITY

What elements or symbols do you envision being part of a community's shared canvas?

How might the image depict the diverse contributions and interactions within a community?

What emotions or experiences do you associate with the belonging of a community?

CANVAS OF COMMUNITY

This image captures an artist at work on a large mural on a city wall, surrounded by a crowd of engaged onlookers. The mural, filled with vibrant colors and themes of cultural and personal significance, becomes a focal point of community interaction. Observers are taking photos and discussing the artwork's themes.

QUESTIONS FOR EXPLORATION

1. **Cultural Reflection:** How does public art reflect the cultural identity of a community?
2. **Artist Influence:** What impact can an artist have on public perception and community engagement through such murals?
3. **Community Engagement:** How does involving the community in the creation of public art affect the relationship between the artwork and its viewers?
4. **Personal Themes:** In what ways can personal themes in public art resonate with diverse audiences?
5. **Urban Art Benefits:** What are the benefits of integrating art into urban spaces?
6. **Viewer Interaction:** How do different forms of interaction from viewers affect their experience of the art?
7. **Artistic Expression:** How does the choice of location influence the themes and execution of a mural?
8. **Civic Pride:** Can public art projects enhance civic pride and cohesion?
9. **Educational Value:** What educational opportunities can public art provide to a community?
10. **Future Projects:** How can cities foster more projects that blend art, culture, and community engagement?

CANVAS OF COMMUNITY

Notes & Reflections

SILENT GREETINGS

What kinds of gestures or expressions do you imagine convey greetings without words?

How might the image depict the subtlety and depth of non-verbal communication?

Have you ever experienced a unique way of greeting someone? If so, what was it?

SILENT GREETINGS

This striking image captures a student with their hands over their mouth, the word 'helo' scribbled on one hand. The blurred background focuses attention on the student's expressive eyes and the message, creating a powerful visual metaphor for communication and identity.

QUESTIONS FOR EXPLORATION

1. **Language and Identity:** How does language shape our identity and the way others perceive us?
2. **Communication Barriers:** What does the gesture of covering the mouth with a 'helo' written on the hand signify about communication barriers?
3. **Non-verbal Expressions:** In what ways can non-verbal expressions complement or contradict spoken language?
4. **Cultural Reflection:** How do linguistic choices reflect cultural and personal identities?
5. **Power of Silence:** Can silence be as powerful a form of communication as words?
6. **Connecting Diverse Groups:** What role does language play in forming connections between diverse groups?
7. **Artistic Exploration:** How can art be used to explore and express issues of language and identity?
8. **Multilingual Challenges:** What are the challenges and benefits of bilingual or multilingual identities?
9. **Color Perception:** How does the use of color in the image influence the perception of the message?
10. **Digital Communication:** What impact might digital communication have on the future of language and identity expression?

SILENT GREETINGS

Notes & Reflections

WORLDS OF WORK

What different work environments or professions do you imagine when you think of the diverse "worlds of work"?

How might the image depict the various cultures and dynamics found within different workplaces?

How can people best adapt to new work settings?

WORLDS OF WORK

This image vividly captures a group of professionals from different fields in their work environments, each deeply engaged in their specialty. The depiction emphasizes the variety of careers and their profound impact on shaping personal and social identities.

QUESTIONS FOR EXPLORATION

1. **Career Impact:** How do different professions shape the personal and social identities of the individuals who practice them?
2. **Diversity Benefits:** What are the benefits of diversity in professional settings?
3. **Professional Challenges:** What unique challenges do professionals face in these varied fields?
4. **Cultural Influence:** How does cultural background influence professional choices and opportunities?
5. **Skill Development:** What skills are common across these professions that contribute to personal growth?
6. **Interdisciplinary Learning:** How can professionals from different fields learn from each other?
7. **Workplace Dynamics:** How does the work environment affect productivity and creativity in these different professions?
8. **Career Advice:** What advice would these professionals likely give to someone entering their field?
9. **Technology's Role:** How is technology shaping the practices in these diverse professions?
10. **Future Trends:** What trends might impact these fields in the next decade?

WORLDS OF WORK

Notes & Reflections

COLORS OF HEALTH

What colors do you associate with different aspects of health and well-being?

How might the image visually represent the concept of health through the use of color?

What do you do to keep healthy?

COLORS OF HEALTH

This vibrant display showcases an array of healthy food choices beautifully arranged on a rustic wooden table in a bright, airy kitchen setting. The vivid colors of the fresh fruits and vegetables create a visually stunning tableau, highlighting the natural beauty and variety of wholesome ingredients.

QUESTIONS FOR EXPLORATION

1. **Nutritional Diversity:** How does eating a variety of colored fruits and vegetables benefit your health?
2. **Meal Preparation:** What are some simple ways to incorporate more vegetables into your everyday meals?
3. **Health Benefits:** Which vitamins and minerals are present in the foods shown in the image, and what are their health benefits?
4. **Kid-Friendly:** How can you make these healthy foods more appealing to children?
5. **Dietary Restrictions:** How can individuals with dietary restrictions (e.g., vegan, gluten-free) ensure they get a balanced diet?
6. **Seasonal Choices:** Which fruits and vegetables in the image are typically in season now, and how does seasonal eating affect nutrition and taste?
7. **Cultural Cuisine:** How can traditional dishes be adapted to include more of these healthy options?
8. **Grocery Shopping:** What tips can you share for selecting the freshest produce at the grocery store?
9. **Eating on a Budget:** How can one maintain a healthy diet without breaking the bank?
10. **Inspiration for Change:** What is one small dietary change you can make today to move towards healthier eating habits?

Notes & Reflections

REFLECTING

WHAT THOUGHTS OR MEMORIES COME TO MIND WHEN YOU THINK ABOUT THE ACT OF REFLECTING?

HOW MIGHT THE IMAGE CAPTURE THE PROCESS OF SELF-REFLECTION OR CONTEMPLATION?

WHAT EMOTIONS OR INSIGHTS DO YOU ASSOCIATE WITH TAKING TIME TO REFLECT ON YOUR EXPERIENCES OR SURROUNDINGS?

REFLECTING

This compelling image captures a student looking into a mirror. On the outside, she embodies a different style with, reflecting a unique personal expression. However, her reflection in the mirror shows her in a traditional school uniform, neat and conventional. This visual raises intriguing questions about the contrast between how we see ourselves and how others perceive us.

QUESTIONS FOR EXPLORATION

1. **Personal vs. Public Identity:** How do you balance your personal identity with how you present yourself in public or at school?
2. **Impact of Appearance:** How might someone's appearance affect the way others perceive their personality or capabilities?
3. **Cultural Expectations:** In what ways do cultural expectations influence how we choose to present ourselves?
4. **Self-expression:** How important is self-expression to you, and what forms does it take in your life?
5. **Misconceptions:** Have you ever been misunderstood because of your appearance or the way you dress?
6. **Peer Pressure:** How does peer pressure influence the way young people like the student in the image choose to dress or behave?
7. **Identity Exploration:** Why might someone choose to present themselves differently at different times or in different settings?
8. **Confidence and Self-Esteem:** How does aligning your outward appearance with your inner self affect your confidence and self-esteem?
9. **Role of Uniforms:** What role do uniforms play in schools or other institutions in shaping or suppressing individual identity?
10. **Changing Perceptions:** How can we encourage a society that values diverse forms of self-expression without judgment?

REFLECTING

Notes & Reflections

ECHOES OF TIME

What memories or historical events come to mind when you think of the echoes of time?

How might the image depict the passage of time and its lingering effects?

What emotions or reflections do you associate with the idea of hearing echoes from the past?

ECHOES OF TIME

This image vividly captures participants dressed in historical attire, reenacting a significant battle or event. The dedication of the participants in bringing history to life not only educates but also fosters a deeper connection with the past, highlighting the cultural and educational importance of historical reenactments.

QUESTIONS FOR EXPLORATION

1. **Authenticity in Reenactment:** How important is authenticity in historical reenactments, and how does it affect the viewer's experience?
2. **Educational Value:** What can individuals learn from participating in or observing a historical reenactment?
3. **Cultural Significance:** How do historical reenactments contribute to preserving cultural heritage?
4. **Public Interest:** What drives the public's interest in watching historical reenactments?
5. **Historical Accuracy:** How do reenactors ensure historical accuracy in their portrayals?
6. **Impact on Historiography:** Can reenactments influence our understanding of history, and if so, how?
7. **Community Involvement:** How do historical reenactments engage and benefit the community?
8. **Personal Connections:** What personal connections do participants often develop with the history they are reenacting?
9. **Costume and Craft:** How do the costumes and craftsmanship contribute to the overall impact of historical reenactments?
10. **Future of Reenactments:** What is the future of historical reenactments in the digital age?

ECHOES OF TIME

Notes & Reflections

LESSON IDEAS

Welcome to the detailed lesson plans section for using this book! Here, you'll find comprehensive and engaging lesson plans designed to maximize the educational value of this book. These plans are tailored to help you effectively convey key concepts, facilitate interactive learning, and ensure a thorough understanding of the material. Whether you're teaching in a classroom setting or facilitating a study group, these structured guides will support you in creating an enriching and dynamic learning experience for your students.

Dive into the lessons and unlock the full potential of this book!

PREDICT THE IMAGE

OBJECTIVES:

- Develop students' predictive skills and critical thinking through image analysis.
- Foster discussion and engagement by using targeted questions to guide predictions about the image.

MATERIALS NEEDED:

- Selected image from the book
- List of guiding questions (the page before the image)
- Notebooks or digital devices for note-taking

PROCEDURE:

1. Guiding Questions and Discussion (20 minutes)

- Use the three questions in the book prior to each image to

PREDICT THE IMAGE

guide the discussion and prompt predictions. You may want to encourage students think about the title.
- Encourage students to share their predictions and thoughts in small groups or pairs.
- Have each group or pair present their predictions to the class, explaining the reasoning behind their ideas.

2. Displaying the Image (5 minutes)

- Show the image in the book or on the screen using the QR code.
- Have students turn and talk to discuss about their predictions, were they correct?

3. Prediction Validation and Exploration (15 minutes)

- Provide background information about the image, by reading the caption.
- Compare the students' predictions with that of the caption and discuss similarities and differences.
- Ask students to reflect on their prediction process and what clues they used to make their guesses.

4. Repeating the Process (30 minutes)

- Repeat the prediction process with the guiding questions.
- Ensure each image is discussed thoroughly, allowing students to practice and improve their predictive skills

5. Creative Writing Activity (Extension Activity)

- Assign a creative writing task where students choose one of the images and write a short story or a descriptive paragraph based on their predictions.

- Encourage them to use descriptive language and incorporate elements from their discussions.

6. Sharing and Feedback (Extension Activity)

- Have students share their written pieces with the class or in small groups.
- Provide constructive feedback and highlight interesting or unique predictions and interpretations.

7. Conclusion and Reflection (10 minutes)

- Summarize the key points discussed during the lesson.
- Reflect on how making predictions can enhance understanding and engagement with visual materials.
- Encourage students to apply these skills when analyzing images in other subjects or contexts.

OBSERVING AND DESCRIBING IMAGES

OBJECTIVE:

Students will enhance their vocabulary and communication skills by making detailed observations of an image and discussing their findings.

MATERIALS:

A detailed image from the "Book of Provocations" (choose an image with rich details and elements that can provoke thought and discussion).

PROCEDURE:

1. **Introduction (5 minutes):**

- Briefly explain the purpose of the lesson: to practice observation skills and descriptive language.
- Discuss why detailed observation is important for communication and understanding.

OBSERVING AND DESCRIBING IMAGES

2. **Image Presentation (5 minutes):**

- Reveal the chosen image to the class.
- Allow students a minute to quietly observe the image.

3. **Observation Activity (10 minutes):**

- Ask students to list approximately ten observations about the image within 3-5 minutes. They should focus on details such as colors, textures, objects, and any interesting elements they notice.
- Encourage the use of descriptive language and expansion of vocabulary by thinking of synonyms and specific terms for what they see.

4. **Sharing Observations (10 minutes):**

- Divide the class into small groups.
- Have each student share their observations with their group.
- Group members should discuss any similarities or differences in their observations and help each other refine their descriptions.

5. **Class Discussion (10 minutes):**

- Bring the class back together and ask each group to share some of their most interesting or unique observations.
- Discuss how these observations can lead to different interpretations or provoke various thoughts.
- Introduce new vocabulary words that came up during the discussion and ensure students understand their meanings.

6. **Reflective Writing (5 minutes):**

- Ask students to spend a few minutes writing a short paragraph about their interpretation of the image based on their observations and the class discussion.

7. **Conclusion (5 minutes):**

- Summarize the key points of the lesson.
- Emphasize the importance of detailed observation and descriptive language in enhancing communication skills.
- Encourage students to apply these observation skills in their everyday lives and other subjects.

CREATIVE WRITING: WRITE THE CAPTION

OBJECTIVE:

Students will enhance their vocabulary and creative writing skills by making detailed observations of an image and re-writing its caption using rich, descriptive language.

MATERIALS

- A detailed image from the "Book of Provocations" • Notebooks or paper for students to write on

- Pens or pencils

PROCEDURE:

1. **Introduction (5 minutes):**

- Briefly explain the purpose of the lesson: to enhance creative writing using descriptive language.

CREATIVE WRITING: WRITE THE CAPTION

- Discuss why detailed observation and rich descriptions are important for effective communication and storytelling.

2. **Image Presentation (5 minutes):**

- Reveal the chosen image to the class.
- Allow students a minute to quietly observe the image.

3. **Mind Map Activity (10 minutes):**

- Ask students to create a mind map of their observations about the image within 3-5 minutes. They should focus on details such as colors, objects, and any interesting elements they notice.
- Encourage students to think of synonyms and specific terms for what they see to expand their vocabulary.

4. **Sharing Observations (10 minutes):**

- Divide the class into small groups.
- Have each student share their observations with their group.
- Group members should discuss any similarities or differences in their observations and help each other refine their descriptions.

5. **Class Discussion (10 minutes):**

- Bring the class back together and ask each group to share some of their most interesting or unique observations.
- Collate any strong vocabulary suggestions shared onto the board.

6. **Creative Writing and Re-writing the Caption (15 minutes):**

- Explain that students will now use their observations to write a new, creative caption for the image. The caption should be rich in descriptive language and capture the essence of the image.
- Provide some examples of creative captions from other images in the book to inspire students.
- Encourage students to be imaginative and use the descriptive language they discussed.

7. **Peer Feedback (10 minutes):**

- Pair students up to share their new captions with each other.
- Instruct each student to provide constructive feedback on their partner's caption, focusing on the use of descriptive language and the effectiveness of the imagery.
- Encourage students to suggest additional adjectives or phrases that could enhance their partner's caption.

8. **Sharing and Reflective Writing (10 minutes):**

- Have students share their improved captions with the class.
- Ask students to spend a few minutes writing a short paragraph about how their interpretation of the image changed after the group discussion, creative writing activity, and peer feedback. Encourage them to reflect on how the use of descriptive language enhanced their writing.

9. **Conclusion (5 minutes):**

- Summarize the key points of the lesson.
- Emphasize the importance of detailed observation and descriptive language in enhancing creative writing skills.

CREATIVE WRITING: WRITE THE CAPTION

- Encourage students to apply these skills in their everyday writing and other subjects.
- Exit Ticket: Have students write one new word they acquired from another students work in the lesson on a sticky note and apply it to the board on the way out.

DEEPER UNDERSTANDING

OBJECTIVES:

- Develop a deeper understanding of the image's subjects.
- Enhance speaking and listening skills through collaborative discussion.

MATERIALS NEEDED:

- An image from the book
- List of provided questions
- Notebooks or digital devices for note-taking

PROCEDURE:

1. **Introduction (10 minutes)**

- Begin by displaying the image to the class.
- Provide a brief overview of the image, highlighting its key elements and context.

DEEPER UNDERSTANDING

2. **Guided Exploration (20 minutes)**

- Use the provided questions from the book to guide students through an in-depth exploration of the image's subjects.

3. **Discussion (30 minutes)**

- Divide students into small groups and assign each group a set of questions.
- Instruct each group to discuss their questions and take notes on their observations and interpretations.
- Encourage students to build upon each other's ideas, fostering a collaborative environment.

4. **Class Presentation (20 minutes)**

- Have each group present their findings to the class.
- Facilitate a class-wide discussion, prompting students to ask questions and provide feedback on each group's presentation.

5. **Conclusion (10 minutes)**

- Summarize the key points discussed during the lesson.
- Highlight how the collaborative discussion helped deepen their understanding of the image's subjects.
- Encourage students to continue exploring and questioning the visual elements they encounter in other images or artworks.

QUESTIONS, QUESTIONS, QUESTIONS

OBJECTIVES:

- Empower students to generate their own questions for deeper inquiry.
- Use the image as a starting point for inquiry-based projects.

MATERIALS NEEDED:

- An image from this book
- Notebooks or digital devices for note-taking

PROCEDURE:

1. Introduction to Inquiry (10 minutes)

- Display the image to the class and briefly discuss its main features and context.
- Explain the importance of asking questions and how it leads to deeper understanding and critical thinking.

2. Question Formulation (20 minutes)

- Encourage students to observe the image closely and jot down any questions that come to mind.
- Provide some example prompts to get them started, such as:
- What story does this image tell?
- What might be happening outside the frame of the image?
- How do the elements in the image relate to each other?
- Give students time to brainstorm and write down their own questions.

3. Sharing and Refining Questions (20 minutes)

- Have students pair up or form small groups to share their questions.
- Encourage them to refine and expand upon each other's questions.
- Guide them in categorizing their questions into themes or topics for further exploration.

4. Planning Inquiry-Based Projects (30 minutes)

- Use the refined questions as a springboard for inquiry-based projects.
- Have each group choose one or two questions to explore in depth.
- Assist students in developing a project plan, including:
- Research methods (e.g., online research, library resources, interviews)
- Presentation format (e.g., report, presentation, creative project)
- Timeline and milestones for completing the project

5. Project Work Time (as needed)

- Allocate time for students to work on their projects, offering guidance and support as needed.
- Encourage them to use various resources and to document their findings and progress.

6. **Presentation and Reflection (class session upon project completion)**

- Have each group present their inquiry-based projects to the class.
- Facilitate a reflection session where students discuss what they learned from the process and how their understanding of the image evolved.

ROLE-PLAYING & DEBATES

OBJECTIVES:

- Encourage students to understand different perspectives by assuming roles related to the image's characters or elements.
- Foster critical thinking and empathy through structured role-playing and debates.

MATERIALS NEEDED:

- An image from this book
- Role description cards or scripts
- Debate guidelines and format

PROCEDURE:

1. Introduction to Role-Playing and Debates (10 minutes)

ROLE-PLAYING & DEBATES

- Display the image to the class and discuss its characters or key elements.
- Explain the concepts of role-playing and debating, and how these activities can help students understand different perspectives and develop critical thinking skills.

2. Role Assignment (10 minutes)

- Assign roles to students based on the image's characters or elements. For example, if the image depicts a historical event, assign roles such as key figures, witnesses, or affected individuals.
- Provide students with role description cards or scripts to help them understand their character's background, motivations, and viewpoints.

3. Preparation for Role-Playing (20 minutes)

- Give students time to research and prepare for their roles. Encourage them to think about their character's perspective and how they might respond to different situations or questions.
- Suggest some questions or scenarios to consider, such as:

What are your character's main goals or concerns?

How does your character view the other characters or elements in the image?

What arguments or evidence might your character use to support their perspective?

4. Role-Playing Activity (30 minutes)

- Organize students into small groups or pairs to engage in role-playing activities. Each group should act out a scenario or discussion based on their assigned roles.
- Encourage students to stay in character and interact with each other, using their research and preparation to guide their responses.

5. **Debate Preparation (15 minutes)**

- Transition from role-playing to debates. Form debate teams based on the different perspectives represented in the image.
- Provide guidelines for the debate, including the format, time limits, and rules for respectful discourse.
- Allow time for teams to prepare their arguments and gather supporting evidence.

6. **Debate Activity (30 minutes)**

- Conduct the debates, with each team presenting their arguments and responding to counterarguments.
- Encourage active listening and critical questioning from both the debaters and the audience.
- Facilitate the debate to ensure that it remains respectful and focused on the topics at hand.

7. **Reflection and Discussion (15 minutes)**

- After the debates, lead a reflection session where students can discuss what they learned from the role-playing and debates.
- Ask questions such as:

  How did taking on a role or participating in a debate change your perspective on the image's subjects?

ROLE-PLAYING & DEBATES

What new insights did you gain about the characters or elements in the image?

How did this activity help you develop empathy and critical thinking skills?

CULTURAL & SOCIAL ANALYSIS

OBJECTIVES:

- Develop an understanding of diverse cultural and social contexts depicted in images.
- Promote global awareness and intercultural understanding through discussion and comparison with students' own experiences

MATERIALS NEEDED:

- A copy of this book
- Selected images depicting various cultural or social contexts
- Notebooks or digital devices for note-taking

PROCEDURE:

1. Introduction to Cultural and Social Contexts (10 minutes)

CULTURAL & SOCIAL ANALYSIS

- Begin by displaying a selection of images that depict different cultural or social settings.
- Provide a brief background on each image, highlighting its cultural or social significance.

2. Image Analysis (20 minutes)

- Divide students into small groups and assign each group an image to analyze.
- Provide guiding questions to help students explore the cultural or social aspects of their assigned image, such as:

What cultural or social elements are present in the image?

How do the subjects in the image interact with their environment?

What traditions, customs, or social norms can you identify?

3. **Group Discussion (30 minutes)**

- Have each group discuss their findings and take notes on their observations.
- Encourage students to draw comparisons between the cultural or social contexts depicted in the images and their own experiences.
- Prompt students to consider questions such as:

How do the cultural or social elements in the image differ from or resemble those in your own community?

What can you learn from the differences and similarities?

4. **Class Presentations (20 minutes)**

- Have each group present their analysis to the class.

- Facilitate a class-wide discussion, encouraging students to ask questions and share their perspectives on the different cultural or social contexts.

5. Promoting Global Awareness (15 minutes)

- Discuss the importance of understanding and appreciating diverse cultures and social contexts.
- Highlight how global awareness and intercultural understanding can foster empathy and reduce stereotypes.
- Encourage students to think about how they can apply what they've learned in their daily lives and interactions with others.

6. Reflection and Writing Activity (15 minutes)

- Ask students to write a brief reflection on what they learned from the lesson.
- Encourage them to consider how the activity has changed their perspective on cultural diversity and social contexts.
- Provide prompts such as:

What new insights did you gain about other cultures or social settings?

How can you use this knowledge to promote understanding and respect in your community?

VOCABULARY BUILDING

NOTE:

These may be used as smaller activities instead of a whole lesson if you think it works better.

OBJECTIVES:

- Expand students' vocabulary through discussion and targeted exercises.

- Reinforce new vocabulary through application in speaking and writing activities.

MATERIALS NEEDED:

- A copy of this book
- Vocabulary lists
- Worksheets for exercises (matching words to definitions, sentence creation, word maps)
- Notebooks or digital devices for note-taking

VOCABULARY BUILDING

- Timer for writing races

PROCEDURE:

1. Introduction to Vocabulary Building (10 minutes)

- Explain the importance of expanding vocabulary and how it enhances communication skills.
- Display the selected image and briefly discuss its main elements and context.

2. Developing Vocabulary Lists (15 minutes)

- During a class discussion, identify key words and phrases related to the image from the book.
- Write these words on the board and ask students to contribute additional relevant words.
- Create a comprehensive vocabulary list based on the discussion.

3. Vocabulary Exercises (20 minutes)

Distribute worksheets with exercises designed to reinforce the new vocabulary, such as:

- Matching words to their definitions
- Using new words in sentences
- Creating word maps that show relationships between words
- Have students complete the exercises individually or in pairs.

4. Application in Speaking Activities (20 minutes)

Organize a speaking activity where students must use the new vocabulary in context. Examples include:

- Partner discussions about the image using as many new words as possible.
- Small group presentations where each student describes a part of the image using the vocabulary list.

5. Application in Writing Activities (20 minutes)

Assign a writing task that requires the use of new vocabulary. Examples include:

- Writing a short story or descriptive paragraph about the image.
- Composing a dialogue between characters in the image, integrating the new words.

6. Writing Races (15 minutes)

Conduct writing races to make vocabulary practice fun and dynamic:

- Set a timer for 3-5 minutes.
- Instruct students to write down as many words related to the image as they can.
- After the time is up, have students share their lists and see who wrote the most words.

7. Review and Reinforcement (10 minutes)

- Review the vocabulary lists and exercises as a class.
- Discuss any challenging words and ensure students understand their meanings and usage.
- Encourage students to continue using these words in their daily conversations and writing assignments.

CREATING AI IMAGES

OBJECTIVE:

Students will enhance their descriptive writing skills by composing clear, detailed, and instructional text to create an image using AI.

MATERIALS:

- A detailed image from the "Book of Provocations" as an example

- Notebooks or paper for students to write on

- Pens or pencils

- Access to an AI image generation tool (e.g., DALL-E, MidJourney)

PROCEDURE:

1. Introduction (5 minutes):

- Briefly explain the purpose of the lesson: to practice using

descriptive and instructional language to create an image with AI.
- Discuss the importance of clear and detailed descriptions for effective communication, especially when giving instructions.

2. Image Presentation (5 minutes):

- Show the chosen image from the "Book of Provocations" to the class.
- Explain that they will be using their descriptive writing skills to produce a similar image using AI.

3. Descriptive Language Warm-Up (10 minutes):

- Conduct a brief warm-up exercise where students practice describing everyday objects in detail.
- Divide students into pairs and give each pair an object (e.g., a book, a plant, a piece of fruit).
- Ask students to take turns describing the object to their partner using as much detail as possible without naming the object. The partner should try to guess what the object is based on the description.
- After a few rounds, discuss the importance of specific and vivid language in descriptions.

4. Writing Descriptions (15 minutes):

- Explain that students will now write a detailed description of the image that includes clear and specific instructions for the AI to follow.
- Provide examples of instructional phrases (e.g., "Create an image of a serene sunset over a calm ocean with vibrant orange and pink hues," "a bustling city street with tall skyscrapers and yellow taxis").

- Encourage students to use their observations and previous descriptions to help.

5. Using AI to Generate Images (15 minutes):

- Have students input their descriptive text into the AI image generation tool.
- Allow students to adjust their descriptions based on the AI-generated images and refine their language to achieve the desired result.
- Encourage students to experiment with different phrases and levels of detail to see how the AI responds.

6. Class Discussion (10 minutes):

- Bring the class back together and ask students to share their AI-generated images and the descriptions they used.
- Discuss the effectiveness of different descriptions and how specific language influenced the AI's output.
- Introduce any new vocabulary words that came up during the activity and ensure students understand their meanings.

7. Reflective Writing (10 minutes):

- Ask students to spend a few minutes writing a short paragraph about their experience using descriptive writing to create an image with AI. Encourage them to reflect on how the use of clear and detailed language enhanced their results.

8. Conclusion (5 minutes):

- Summarize the key points of the lesson.

- Emphasize the importance of detailed and clear descriptions in enhancing communication skills, especially when giving instructions.
- Encourage students to apply these skills in their everyday writing and other subjects.

COLLABORATIVE STORIES

OBJECTIVE:

Students will develop their creative writing, collaboration, and storytelling skills by creating a collaborative story inspired by images from the "Book of Provocations."

MATERIALS:

- Multiple detailed images from "A Book of Provocations"
- Notebooks or paper for students to write on
- Pens or pencils
- A large sheet of paper or whiteboard for collaborative story mapping

PROCEDURE:

1. Introduction (5 minutes):

COLLABORATIVE STORIES

- Briefly explain the purpose of the lesson: to collaboratively create a story inspired by images and enhance creative writing and teamwork skills.
- Discuss the elements of a good story (e.g., setting, characters, conflict, resolution) and how images can serve as inspiration for storytelling.

2. Image Selection (5 minutes):

- Display several images from the "Book of Provocations" around the classroom.
- Allow students to walk around and choose an image that particularly inspires them.
- Divide students into small groups based on the image they choose, ensuring each group has a different image.

3. Brainstorming Session (10 minutes):

- In their groups, students will brainstorm ideas for a story inspired by their chosen image.
- Encourage them to think about the setting, characters, and potential plot points that the image suggests.
- Each group should create a mind map or list of ideas on a large sheet of paper.

4. Story Mapping (10 minutes):

- Provide each group with a large sheet of paper or use a section of the whiteboard.
- Have each group outline their story using a story map, including the introduction, rising action, climax, falling action, and resolution.
- Encourage groups to think about how their story will progress and ensure it has a clear structure.

5. Collaborative Writing (20 minutes or as needed):

- Each group will work together to write their story, using the story map as a guide.
- Assign roles within each group (e.g., one student writes the introduction, another writes the climax, etc.) to ensure everyone contributes.
- Encourage students to use descriptive language and vivid imagery inspired by their chosen image.

6. Illustrating the Story (10 minutes):

- After writing the story, each group will create an illustration that represents a key scene or the overall theme of their story.
- Provide drawing materials and encourage creativity in their illustrations.

7. Story Sharing (15 minutes):

- Bring the class back together and have each group present their story and illustration to the class.
- Encourage students to give positive feedback and ask questions about each group's story.

8. Class Discussion (10 minutes):

- Discuss how the images from "A Book of Provocations" inspired different stories and creative ideas.
- Talk about the importance of collaboration and how working together can enhance creativity and storytelling.
- Highlight any new vocabulary or descriptive language used in the stories and ensure students understand their meanings.

9. Reflective Writing (5 minutes):

- Ask students to spend a few minutes writing a short paragraph about their experience of creating a collaborative story. Encourage them to reflect on what they enjoyed, any challenges they faced, and how they contributed to the group.

10. Conclusion (5 minutes):

- Summarize the key points of the lesson.
- Emphasize the importance of creativity, collaboration, and descriptive language in storytelling.
- Encourage students to use these skills in future writing projects and other collaborative activities.

CONCLUSION

Thank you for joining me on this journey through **A Book of Provocations**. I hope these pages have challenged your perspectives, ignited thoughtful discussions, and inspired meaningful action in your life and work. This collection of provocations was crafted to stimulate deep thinking and encourage you to question the status quo, pushing the boundaries of conventional wisdom.

As we conclude this volume, I am excited to share that A Book of Provocations is an ongoing project. Future volumes will continue to explore new themes, present fresh images, and pose new questions designed to provoke thought and inspire change. Each new installment will delve deeper into the complexities of our world, offering you more opportunities to engage with compelling ideas and perspectives.

To stay updated on upcoming volumes and other exciting news, please visit my website regularly. You'll find the latest information, announcements, and exclusive content that you won't want to miss.

CONCLUSION

Additionally, I invite you to subscribe to my newsletter. By joining the newsletter community, you will receive new lesson plans and tools designed to complement the content of A Book of Provocations. These resources will help you integrate the book's ideas into your teaching, discussions, and personal growth practices.

Don't forget to follow my social media accounts for real-time updates, thought-provoking content, and a chance to engage with a community of like-minded individuals. Your support and engagement are invaluable as we continue this journey together.

Thank you for being part of this project. I look forward to exploring new horizons with you in future volumes. Stay curious, continue to question, and let the provocations lead you to new insights.

With gratitude,

Matt Fletcher

ALSO BY MATT FLETCHER

It's Alwrite! A Practical Guide to Writing Different Text Types in English

Are you ready to master the art of writing in English? Whether you're a student, educator, or writing enthusiast, "It's Alwrite!" is your comprehensive guide to understanding and crafting a wide array of English text types.

Each chapter delves into the unique features of a different text type (18 in the book), offering you essential tips and suggestions, clear formatting guidelines, and real-world examples. To help you practice and perfect your writing, each text includes prompts and exercises tailored to each text type.

"It's Alwrite!" is a great resource for students and teachers of the International Baccalaureate English B Language Acquisition Course, but it's not just for IB students. Designed to be your go-to resource for writing with confidence and clarity, no matter the occasion or audience, this book will help you unlock your writing potential and make your words work for you!

Available now on Amazon and other retailers or visit http://www.matttfletcher.com for more information.

ABOUT THE AUTHOR

MATT FLETCHER

Originally from the U.K., Matt Fletcher has taught internationally for over ten years, enriching his educational methods with diverse cultural insights. With extensive experience in both education and leadership, he excels at mentoring, coaching, and motivating students and professionals alike. Committed to promoting inclusive and collaborative atmospheres, Matt is passionate about creating learning environments that foster curiosity and providing resources that enable both teachers and students to excel and thrive. You can connect with Matt via his website at matttfletcher.com or follow him on social media at @matttfletcher.

- instagram.com/matttfletcher
- linkedin.com/in/matttfletcher
- threads.net/@matttfletcher

www.ingramcontent.com/pod-product-compliance
Lightning Source LLC
Chambersburg PA
CBHW070537010526
44118CB00012B/1161